MW00471609

A truly life-transfor.
learn how to take control of your decisions, you
need to read this book.

—KAREN KOTTARIDIS
CHANCELLOR
WAGNER LEADERSHIP INSTITUTE

Clear, practical, biblical teaching filled with gold
nuggets of insight into the realm of spiritual
warfare. If you have internal struggles when you
make decisions, this book is for you.

—PASTOR SHIRLENE MOORE
SENIOR PASTOR
WORD OF LOVE CHRISTIAN CENTER
HURST, TX

Karen has written a great book to open our eyes
to the unseen world that influences us on a daily
basis. I like the fact that believers and non-believers
will be able to understand it and get something
out of it. I highly recommend this book!

—BRENDA EAGANS
PROPHETIC EVANGELIST
HEART OF GOD MINISTRIES
NORTH RICHLAND HILLS, TX

Life
in the
MATRIX

KAREN BLANKS ADAMS

CREATION
HOUSE
A STRANG COMPANY

LIFE IN THE MATRIX by Karen Blanks Adams
Published by Creation House
A Strang Company
600 Rinehart Road
Lake Mary, Florida 32746
www.strangbookgroup.com

This book or parts thereof may not be reproduced in any form, stored in a retrieval system, or transmitted in any form by any means—electronic, mechanical, photocopy, recording, or otherwise—without prior written permission of the publisher, except as provided by United States of America copyright law.

Unless otherwise noted, all Scripture quotations are from the Holy Bible, New International Version of the Bible. Copyright © 1973, 1978, 1984, International Bible Society. Used by permission.

Scripture quotations marked KJV are from the King James Version of the Bible.

Scripture quotations marked NKJV are from the New King James Version of the Bible. Copyright © 1979, 1980, 1982 by Thomas Nelson, Inc., publishers. Used by permission.

Scripture quotations marked AMP are from the Amplified Bible. Old Testament copyright © 1965, 1987 by the Zondervan Corporation. The Amplified New Testament copyright © 1954, 1958, 1987 by the Lockman Foundation. Used by permission.

Scripture quotations marked NAS are from the New American Standard Bible. Copyright © 1960, 1962, 1963, 1968, 1971, 1972, 1973, 1975, 1977 by the Lockman Foundation. Used by permission. (www.Lockman.org)

Design Director: Bill Johnson

Cover design by Justin Evans

Copyright © 2010 by Karen Blanks Adams
All rights reserved

Library of Congress Control Number: 2010926532
International Standard Book Number: 978-1-61638-170-7

First Edition

10 11 12 13 14 — 9 8 7 6 5 4 3 2 1
Printed in the United States of America

Dedicated to

My adoring husband, Leeman;

Our son, Alex;

Our parents;

Our sisters and brothers;

Our nieces and nephews; and to

All future generations in the ages to come.

May your eyes be enlightened

To see beyond the obvious,

Overcome the darkness, and

Behold the goodness of the Lord.

Contents

Foreword

IN 1978, AS A TWENTY-FOUR-YEAR-OLD Christian in a denominational church, I first embraced this fundamental truth: the devil is a liar, and he does not want me to experience the love and power of the Lord Jesus Christ. Since becoming a Christian as a teenager, I had known, intellectually, that the devil exists. I just did not give him much thought, and I certainly did not think he spent much time worrying about me.

All that changed, however, when the devil whispered one little lie into my ear in a moment of weakness and loss. At two o'clock in the morning, a phone call shattered my sleep with the news that a dear friend had been killed in a car accident. As grief flooded my body, the enemy of my soul said, "She's just dead. There is no eternal life." Although I immediately rejected the lie in my mind, the seed of doubt had been planted. Unknown to me at that time, the seed would germinate in darkness and grow into a tree of unbelief.

The next eighteen months were the darkest of my life. Inch by inch, the enemy's seed grew until every part of my being had been infiltrated by doubt and fear. Ultimately, I was spiritually and mentally crippled by unbelief to the point that I was seriously contemplating suicide. The devil had planted despair in my life, and I was reaping the fruit of depression and hopelessness.

But God is good, and He had no intention of leaving me alone in that dark place. One day, with no hope in sight, God pulled back the veil of lies and revealed the origin of my desperation. My good and loving Father took me back to that moment right after the phone call when the enemy's voice whispered in my ear. The Lord showed me that rejecting a lie with the power of my mind is not enough; I had to wage war against my enemy with the power and authority of the Holy Spirit.

So I did. In that moment, with my husband by my side, I confessed my sin of entertaining and receiving a diabolical lie from the devil. By faith, I rejected the lie and received the truth from my Lord and Savior, Jesus Christ—that the gift of God is eternal life. For the next twelve months, every time the enemy whispered in my ear, I yelled back with the Word of God. I learned more about spiritual warfare in those twelve months than in my entire life up to that point!

Make no mistake, the devil is a liar, and he does not want you to experience the love and power of the Lord Jesus Christ. This book by Karen Adams, *Life in the Matrix,* can be a weapon in your arsenal as you wage your own war against the enemy of your soul. You too can fight the good fight and experience abundant—and victorious—life.

—PAM PIERCE
COAUTHOR, *THE REWARDS OF SIMPLICITY*

Acknowledgments

FIRST AND FOREMOST, I WANT to thank the Lord God Almighty for placing this project upon my heart. This book would not have been possible without the Lord opening my mind to consider the possibility of spiritual forces influencing our daily lives.

While writing this book, I would often say, "My next book will be titled, Downloads from God," because throughout this assignment, I always received the right amount of revelation at the right time. At no point did I experience writer's block, confusion, or frustration. And, I learned so much.

I will be forever grateful to the many people who taught me without knowing it through their books, magazines, DVDs, and other forms of media. As I gathered materials to do my research, I was amazed at the number of books and articles that have been written on spiritual warfare. I want to thank my publisher, Creation House, and the owners, Stephen and Joy Strang, for having the faith in this project to publish it. I also want to thank their team of editors and artists whose talent, skills, and abilities are used every day for the glory of God.

Special thanks to Dr. Chuck and Pam Pierce for their love and support. I will never be able to express the joy they bring into my life through their faithful, tireless efforts to advance the kingdom of God through Glory of Zion International Ministries. Pam, thanks so much for writing the foreword to this book. I appreciate you more than words can say.

I also want to thank Dr. C. Peter and Doris Wagner and the entire faculty and staff of Wagner Leadership Institute for the remarkably insightful training they offer. You made it easy and enjoyable for me to learn.

And to Dr. Robert and Dr. Linda Heidler, two of the most anointed teachers I know, thank you for your carefully researched, scholarly training. I have learned so much from your sermons, seminars, and the Issachar School. Thank you for making your classes available on CD and DVD. They are a treasure that I will always cherish.

Thank you to Pastors Ronnie and Shirlene Moore, Reverend David and Donna McGraw, Brenda Eagans, Karen Kottaridis, and Kathy Ide for reading my manuscripts and providing edits, comments, and wise counsel.

Most of all, I want to thank my husband, Leeman; our son, Alex; my mother, Shirley Lynch; my sisters, Sharon Jones, Crystal Blanks, and Aliceia Gordon; and my brother, Markus Lynch, for their encouragement and unfailing love.

May grace, peace, love, and prosperity be yours in abundance always.

Introduction

*H*AVE YOU EVER GIVEN ADVICE to someone and later thought, *Why did I say that?* Have you ever done something and later wondered, *Why did I do that?* Or have you ever known someone who did something so completely out of character that it seemed unexplainable? We often hear people say, "It's easy to have 20/20 vision after the fact." Others may call this hindsight "Monday morning quarterbacking." Whatever we call it, we can all remember times in our lives when we did something out of the ordinary and questioned it afterwards.

Every day we make decisions based on our instincts, experiences, knowledge, and wisdom. We may attribute our innate decision-making skills to our intuition, our conscience, our childhood, or our education. We might be swayed by our prejudices, biases, traditions, or other preconceived beliefs. Or we could be influenced by our friends and family. At other times, an inner voice guides us. Whatever the basis for our rationale, most of us believe we are in control of our actions when we give advice or make choices.

In the Warner Brothers movie *The Matrix*, a computer program controls everyone's activities, but the people who live in the Matrix are unaware of the program's existence. In real life, we go about our daily lives making decisions we believe are based on our own reasoning and on the external guidance we have obtained from others. No matter what variables contribute to our decision-making process, ultimately we believe we are in control of our actions. Yet often people do things completely out of character that shock their family and friends. Society is quick to attribute these acts to "poor judgment" or "temporary insanity."

But are we dismissing these acts too quickly? Are the explanations we commonly offer for misfortune, inappropriate behavior, unacceptable conduct, and atrocious acts our way of trying to logically explain the unexplainable? Is it possible we are being influenced by unseen forces? Is it possible we are not in control?

Supernatural Forces

The concept of supernatural forces is difficult to comprehend. It certainly is not a topic about which I ever thought I would write. However, sometimes things happen in our lives that cause us to seek new revelation on what we believe. In my case, my quest to understand the supernatural began with a difference of opinion.

A friend and I had a disagreement concerning his son that caused me to research the biblical principle of spiritual warfare. My friend believes we need to look beyond the person to discern the spiritual forces at work behind a person's actions. He believes spiritual opponents can and do cause people to behave in certain ways.

My friend's son was away attending college, and he was unemployed. My friend told me his son had become hesitant about leaving his apartment, even to attend classes. He had trouble developing new friendships, and he struggled with a lack of self-confidence. My friend said he believed a demon was causing his son to feel immobilized and fearful and was hindering him from finding a job.

I disagreed. I told him the reason his son wasn't working was that he wasn't seriously looking for a job, and the reason he was staying in his apartment was that he enjoyed hanging out with his roommates and playing music. "As long as you continue to completely support him and pay all his expenses," I said, "he has no incentive to work." My friend accused me of looking at the situation only with worldly wisdom. He told me I was not exercising spiritual discernment.

I am a human resources manager, and I admit I had never given any thought to the possibility that demons could be a reason for a person not finding a job. My "worldly wisdom" would attribute their lack of success to being lazy, to not trying hard enough, to being too picky, to not pursuing the right opportunities, or to some other controllable reason.

After our discussion, I began to wonder if I did lack spiritual discernment in this area. I have attended church most of my life. However, the topic of demons controlling us or influencing our daily lives had never been addressed in a sermon.

THE DEVIL MADE ME DO IT

As a human resources manager, I deal with cause-and-effect scenarios daily in the workplace. If you steal from your company and are caught doing it, you're going to be fired, no matter how long you have worked for the company. Employees counseled for inappropriate behavior in the workplace often blame their actions on depression, anxiety, addictions, stress, or some other physical or emotional malady.

In some instances, the employees are not able to offer any reasonable explanation for their inappropriate behavior. This reminds me of the old Flip Wilson television show—whenever he would get in trouble, he would say, "The devil made me do it." Although that was his punch line and it made us laugh, is it possible that we lack spiritual discernment and that demonic forces really are influencing people's everyday actions? Is it possible that, in some cases, the devil did make them do it?

Our society is fascinated by the paranormal, as evidenced by the array of articles, books, movies, and television programs that exist concerning unexplainable phenomenon. People from all countries, cultures, and belief systems seek to understand whether spiritual beings exist. This book, *Life in the Matrix*, examines the existence and influence of spiritual beings from a biblical perspective. Although the Bible is the primary source of reference, this book is intended for both Christians and non-Christians because we are all impacted by internal struggles when making decisions.

In Ephesians 6:12, we read, "For our struggle is not against flesh and blood, but against the rulers, against the authorities, against the powers of this dark world and against the spiritual forces of evil in the heavenly realms." *Life in the Matrix* explores whether the spiritual warfare taking place in the heavenly realms has a direct impact on our day-to-day lives.

Examples are cited throughout the book from current events and news stories to illustrate possible instances of supernatural forces influencing people's actions. Points are driven home with anecdotes about real people who made decisions that negatively impacted their lives or the lives of others. For each example, this book discusses the interrelationship of these events, contrasting possible natural and supernatural causes.

This book challenges its readers to consider the possibility that spiritual forces of evil are influencing their decisions and controlling their lives. It brings to light the root causes of our internal struggles with thoughts, feelings, and actions that are not compatible with our values and beliefs, and it offers strategies to maintain control.

Even readers who don't believe in God or in angels, demons, and the devil may find themselves wondering, *Am I in control of my decisions? Or am I living my life in the Matrix?*

A Servant's Prayer

I have continually sought wisdom and understanding through prayer and from the Word of God to write a scripturally sound book that will be beneficial to and easily understood by a wide audience. I pray this book will awaken people to consider the possibility that spiritual warfare is real and supernatural forces can influence our everyday decisions. I pray the strategies provided in this book for triumphing over demonic forces and living victorious lives are helpful to its readers.

Francis Bacon once said of lofty writers, "Their discourses are as the stars which give little light, because they are so high."[1] My aim in writing has been just the opposite. I have strived to bring clarity to the biblical principle of spiritual warfare by citing actual examples of unexplainable events that could have been caused by demonic supernatural forces. I have endeavored to shine light into the darkness by writing a very quick and easy-to-read book that will dispel fears and offer hope and practical guidance to its readers on how to confidently handle life's challenges.

Blaise Pascal (1623–1662), one of the great seventeenth-century scientists and mathematicians, wrote in his perennial best-seller *Pensées* as follows: "Eloquence is an art of saying things in such a way (1) that those to whom we speak may listen to them without pain and with pleasure; (2) that they feel themselves interested, so that self-love leads them more willingly to reflection upon it."[2] It is my prayer that I have written with the eloquence needed to provide enlightenment on my subject. I pray this book appeals to your senses and fills you with encouragement and the revelation knowledge you need to understand and overcome spiritual attacks.

The purpose of this book is twofold: (1) to expose what may be the underlying cause of internal struggles, and (2) to provide strategies to triumph over them. God has wonderful plans for us, as He declares in Jeremiah 29:11: "'For I know the plans I have for you,' declares the LORD, 'plans to prosper you and not to harm you, plans to give you hope and a future.'" He wants us to have a prosperous, bright future. By understanding the forces that may be influencing our decisions, we will be able to take control of our everyday choices and live victorious lives!

A LAYMAN'S CONFESSION

I do believe that Christ Jesus is the Lord and Savior of this world and that the devil is trying to do everything he can to thwart the kingdom of God. However, I must admit, at the time I began to write this book I doubted the existence of demons who influence our everyday decisions. But as I continued to write, I was forced to ask myself whether my ears had been closed to hear and my eyes had been blinded to see the truth.

After reading this book, I would like to hear from you. What are your thoughts on spiritual warfare? Are your day-to-day decisions your own or are they divinely influenced? Do you believe in spiritual manifestations in the earthly realm? Is it possible we are not fully in control of ourselves? These are thought-provoking questions. I invite you to go to www.lifeinthematrix.com to tell me about your experiences and answer the question, Am I in control, or am I living my life in the Matrix?

1

The Battle Within

W E HAVE ALL FACED MOMENTS of indecision. We have all made decisions that we later questioned. We have all behaved in ways that we later regretted. In the Book of Romans, the apostle Paul reveals his struggle to master himself: "I do not understand what I do. For what I want to do I do not do, but what I hate I do....For I have the desire to do what is good, but I cannot carry it out. For what I do is not the good I want to do; no, the evil I do not want to do—this I keep on doing" (Rom. 7:15, 18–19).

This scripture was written approximately two thousand years ago, yet it clearly describes the internal conflict we sometimes have when making decisions. We are often torn between what we should do, what we want to do, and what we end up doing. At times, like the apostle Paul, the evil we do not want to do is what we do.

The question of how and why we make certain choices has challenged mankind for centuries. There are divergent opinions on why we do what we do. Philosophers, theologians, scholars, and scientists have debated this question since ancient times but have been unable to agree on an explanation for the often mystifying behavior of human beings. Aristotle (384–322 BCE) wrote in his *Posterior Analytics*, "To know a thing's nature is to know the reason why it is."[1] Using Aristotle's logic, if we can understand the nature of evil, we may be able to unravel the mystery behind our internal struggles.

Philosophical Theories About Human Reason

Aristotle is widely regarded as one of the most influential philosophers of all time. He made lasting contributions in many areas of study, such as logic, metaphysics, and ethics, and he pioneered the notion of causality. He is known for formalizing deductive logic and for expressing the law of cause and effect. The law of cause and effect is the foundation upon which later philosophers and scientists have built theories of causation used to study human reason. Cause and effect is a process of logical deduction based on drawing inferences from everyday observations or experiences.

One of the philosophers who adapted Aristotle's theories concerning causation was the medieval philosophical theologian Thomas Aquinas (1225–1274). Thomas Aquinas is most known for his theological classic *Summa Theologiae*, a volume of books that "provides the framework for Catholic studies in systematic theology and for a classical Christian philosophy."[2]

Aquinas spent the final nine years of his life writing the *Summa Theologiae*. In volume two, he composed an argument for the existence of God, claiming: "There are five ways in which one can prove that there is a God."[3] The focal point of the "second way" is the relationship between cause and effect. In his discussion on cause and effect, Aquinas concentrates on the cause behind each effect and seeks to understand the origin of this causal chain. Believing that a series of causes must stop somewhere, or else extend into infinity—which is not possible—he concludes that the first cause must be God. Aquinas concludes God is the first cause because all things were made by God.[4] Does this mean God is the cause of evil? No, absolutely not! God hates evil. God cannot be tempted by evil, nor does He tempt anyone or cause anyone to do evil. God created everything to be good, yet evil exists.

This begs the question, What is the cause of evil on Earth? A comprehensive response to this question is discussed throughout this book, along with real-life guidance on how to triumph over evil. But before diving into that, it might be helpful to explore some alternative views on human reasoning.

Blaise Pascal, mentioned above, developed the theory of probability, which forever changed the way we regard risk, uncertainty, and the decision-making process. Probability theory is designed to study the likelihood of a particular event occurring in a series of random events, in order to predict future outcomes or (in the case of human beings) behavior. Probability mathematics can effectively assess the probable outcomes of many of our choices. Insurance companies use it to establish life expectancy actuarial tables for high-risk people, such as cigarette smokers. Law enforcement uses it to solve serial crimes since habitual criminals frequently follow predictable patterns. Gamblers use it to try to beat the odds in casinos, especially in card games, because they can determine the probability of what cards will be dealt based on knowing what cards have already been played.

As children, we were taught to consider the probable consequences of our actions using if/then scenarios. We know that if we are caught breaking the law, then we will probably go to jail. Children are taught to discern between good and evil, right and wrong, by considering the end result of their decisions. When considering various options, an understanding of the probable outcome of each can be a very useful decision-making tool.

Another philosopher, Immanuel Kant (1724–1804), viewed cause and effect as structured categories built on observations that our minds process into logical concepts.[5] *Process-mapping* is a modern-day example of this methodical view of cause and effect. Process-mapping is used in many corporations to visually review and understand their processes in order to make improvements. It is a useful method for distinguishing what people perceive they are doing from what they are actually doing. By mapping our observations into structured categories, our minds can process what we are doing and develop logical models to achieve results. Kant understood the power of perception. Kant concluded that our perceptions are derived from our judgments and that the purpose of looking for a cause for any given effect is to satisfy our need for an intelligible, ordered world.[6] Kant's theory could lead us to conclude that evil is only what we, as individuals, are capable of perceiving it to be based on our own understanding of right and wrong. Perception can be a barrier to receiving new revelation.

Another theory, the attribution theory, developed by the Austrian-born U.S. psychologist Fritz Heider (1896–1988), is concerned with the ways in which people explain and the motives to which people attribute the behavior of others and themselves. In his book *The Psychology of Interpersonal Relations*, Heider discusses the phenomena of, "How one person thinks and feels about another person, how he perceives him and what he does to him, what he expects him to do or think, and how he reacts to the actions of the other." He narrows the scope of this topic in his book to "the events that occur in everyday life on a conscious level, rather than with the unconscious processes....These intuitively understood and 'obvious' human relations can, as we shall see, be just as challenging and psychologically significant as the deeper and stranger phenomena."[7] Throughout the book, case studies depict human behavior. On the one hand, a person's behavior can be attributed to internal, dispositional causes if the person's behavior is different from how others behave but consistent with his or her own past behavior. And, on the other hand, a person's behavior is attributable to external causes if it is similar to other people in the same situation but inconsistent with that person's own past behavior. This theory leaves us asking, To what should we attribute behavior that is inconsistent not only with that person's past behavior but also with that of other people in similar circumstances? Could supernatural forces be the cause?

We have all made ill-advised, impulsive decisions that we later questioned because they were uncharacteristic of us or inconsistent with our normal tendencies. Some scientists theorize that behavioral impulses are unconsciously activated prior to conscious awareness and that therefore they are the underlying cause of our actions.[8] According to this theory, impulsive behavior originates in our subconscious mind and prompts us into action without our control. This theory, however, leaves unanswered the question, What is the underlying cause of these behavioral impulses? We will look at one possible explanation when we consider the nature of evil.

The above theories and philosophies are a very limited sample of the array of views shared by philosophers and scientists concerning human reasoning. Despite centuries of thought by a multitude of people, we still don't know for certain the cause of human behavior.

Uncaused Cause

Since the 1800s, there have been new developments in the areas of hypnotism and evolutionary theory that center on the possibility of unconscious, unintended causes for human behavior. Recent research conducted at Yale University offers new scientific insight into the unconscious mind that may provide a possible explanation for human behavior.

One possible explanation for people's unexplainable behavior was offered in an article by Benedict Carey titled "Who's Minding the Mind" published in the *New York Times* on July 31, 2007. The article is based on an interview with a professor of psychology at Yale University, Dr. John A. Bargh, the director of the Yale

Automaticity in Cognition, Motivation, and Evaluation (ACME) Laboratory. The research conducted at the lab focuses on the unconscious or automatic ways in which our current environmental surroundings cause us to think, feel, and behave without our conscious intention or knowledge.

Based on their studies, which are supported by past scientific research compiled and examined by personnel at ACME, Bargh and his colleagues have come to believe that unconscious, automatic processes play a role in human behavior that may be responsible for stereotyping and prejudice. They believe these processes may also affect social demeanors such as aggression and politeness and determine whether we like or dislike certain people, places, and things.[9]

According to the news article, one reason for "how we can be generous one moment and petty the next, or act rudely at a dinner party when convinced we are emanating charm" may be "because our subconscious brain is capable of independently choosing what we are going to do."[10] Dr. Bargh claims we have "unconscious behavior guidance systems that are continually furnishing suggestions through the day about what to do next, and the brain is considering and often acting, all before conscious awareness."[11] Dr. Bargh said sometimes these actions "are in line with our conscious intentions and purposes, and sometimes they're not."[12]

This research provides scientific insight into the dynamics of decision-making and reveals how active, purposeful, and independent our subconscious brain is in making choices. Although this article offers just one of many scientific explanations for our unexplainable behavior, it also opens the door to consideration of what may be causing our subconscious brain to be at odds with our conscious intentions and purposes. After discussing the significance of choice, we will consider one possible explanation for this disconnect.

CHOICE

Oftentimes, we know that what we want to do is not what we should do. Choice is a key aspect of the internal conflicts that arise when making decisions. In the book *Choose!*, authors Dottie Gandy and Marsha Clark state that the most powerful tool we have at our disposal is a "tool called choice." They tell us it is our "ally in the best of times" and our "resource in the most challenging times." They go on to say, "All of us are called upon to make dozens, perhaps hundreds, of choices every day. Some choices have little impact, while others have significant impact, on the direction and quality of our lives." In their book, they recognize the struggles we face every day and offer guidance on "how to make intentional and thoughtful choices, even 'on the run,' such that our lives and those around us are positively impacted."[13]

Inherently, most of us want to make decisions that positively impact our lives and the lives of those around us; however, we have the free will to choose to do otherwise. This freedom to choose permits us to make intentional, thoughtful choices every day. It also permits us to make choices inconsistent with our values and beliefs, choices that we later regret.

At times, we may opt for the easy way rather than the right way and then rationalize our actions in the belief that the end justifies the means. An example of the long-lasting consequences of making choices while focused only on the end result can be seen in the following case.

In December 2008, a major affinity Ponzi scheme perpetrated by Bernard L. Madoff was revealed that involved the mismanagement of billions of investment dollars worldwide. Investors chose to invest with Madoff's company because it continually produced higher than average returns, even during global economic downturns. Many of them also elected to do business with him because they believed he shared their values and beliefs. As a result, many foundations, philanthropists, trusts, and financial firms suffered huge losses. In his plea allocution to the court, Madoff said, "I felt compelled to satisfy my clients at any cost." He said he had every intention of terminating the scheme, but it proved "difficult, and ultimately impossible."[14] This case illustrates the importance of considering the cost of our choices to ourselves and others.

We may know what we should do but might still be enticed to do something else. If it seems too good to be true, it probably is. Every choice we make has real and potentially long-lasting consequences.

Free Will

A group of Greek philosophers, the Stoics, who debated with the apostle Paul in the Bible (Acts 17:18) believed individuals are ultimately in control of their own lives. They believed no person or force of nature could control the inner life; people had the free will to choose. *The American Heritage College Dictionary* defines *free will* as "the power of making free choices that are unconstrained by external circumstances or by an agency such as fate or divine will."[15] The concept of free will is fundamental to God's plan for creation.

When God created the earth, He gave man dominion over it. In Genesis 1:28, we read, "Then God blessed them, and God said to them, 'Be fruitful and multiply; fill the earth and subdue it; have dominion over the fish of the sea, over the birds of the air, and over every living thing that moves on the earth'" (NKJV).

When God gave us dominion, He gave us the right to make our own decisions. This is called free will. Adam and Eve could choose to eat from the tree of the knowledge of good and evil. They decided to disobey God and listen to the serpent. Because of their choice, all human beings have, in essence, partaken of the tree of the knowledge of good and evil. We too have the free will to choose to follow either godly wisdom or worldly wisdom. And, like Adam and Eve, we must live with the consequences of our choices.

God gives us boundaries. Bad things can happen if we step outside those boundaries. God will not always prevent Satan's attacks if we live recklessly, without regard to godly wisdom. We are taught by God through the Bible, the Holy Spirit, our experiences, and our relationships with others how to make wise choices.

The free will doctrine is often used to explain willful acts of evil, as well as the love of God. According to this doctrine, God gives us the freedom to choose because He loves us. We can choose to love and trust Him, or we can choose not to. We can choose to do good, or we can choose to do evil. God wants us to make decisions that positively impact our lives and the lives of others, but He has given us the freedom to make decisions with negative consequences as well.

Are We in Control?

We began this chapter with the following scripture: "What I want to do I do not do" (Rom. 7:15). Sometimes, despite ourselves, we choose to follow the wrong path. Some choices we make, we don't intend to make. At other times, we may consciously choose to do something we know we should not do. What could cause us to make decisions that could potentially harm us or thwart our future success?

The theories, philosophies, and doctrines cited above offer some explanations for human behavior from a natural perspective. However, philosophical dogmas tend to avoid teachings that mankind might deem illogical. Generally, they do not venture into the supernatural realm. The remainder of this book will consider human behavior, specifically irrational or unexplainable behavior, from a supernatural perspective using the Holy Bible as the primary source of reference. It will delve into the issue of spiritual warfare and consider the possibility of the existence of spiritual beings that influence our day-to-day actions. It will examine the impact of spiritual warfare on both Christians and non-Christians, because we are all inclined to do or say something that we question afterwards. Are we in control of our decisions? Or are we living our life in the Matrix?

Spiritual Deception

*T*HE IDEA THAT PEOPLE MAY be unconsciously yielding their authority to unseen supernatural forces is hard to believe. However, it can be demonstrated by considering how emotions impact human behavior. Emotions can be controlling and deceptive. At times, we believe we understand the rationale behind the expression of our emotions. At other times, our emotions confuse us.

According to *The American Heritage Desk Dictionary, emotion* is defined as "a mental condition marked by excitement or stimulation of the passions or sensibilities; or, a strong complex feeling."[1] Emotions are subjective and can be influenced by many factors. Examples of emotions include love, hate, joy, and rage. They can be expressed either through physical outbursts, such as laughter and tears, or through our actions, such as participating in a protest rally or voting for certain political candidates and referendums.

Depending on our level of commitment and involvement in a decision, our emotions can impact, consciously or unconsciously, how we react. Our commitment is linked to our expectations. Our expectations are linked to our desires. And our desires are linked to our emotions. Emotions are complex, invisible mental states that often influence our behavior. Is it beyond the realm of possibility that we may be influenced at times by other unseen forces? Is it possible that supernatural forces or evil spirits are, at times, taking advantage of our emotions?

The reality of evil spirits or demons is not readily accepted in Western cultures. Somehow people have been convinced that the devil is a cartoon character or a philosophical metaphor for evil. The devil is often depicted as a man dressed in a red suit carrying a pitchfork. His name is attached to products, such as the Dirt Devil vacuum cleaner; to athletic teams, such as the New Jersey Devils; and to school mascots, such as the one for the Duke Blue Devils. These inaccurate portrayals transform a formidable foe into something to be desired or revered. Such depictions blind society and permit the devil and his demons (evil spirits) to exploit this worldview unnoticed. How can they do this?

Evil spirits can manifest themselves through our emotions disguised as phobias. A phobia is defined in *The American Heritage College Dictionary* as "a persistent, abnormal or irrational fear of a specific thing or situation that compels one to avoid it, despite the awareness that it is not dangerous."[2] A spirit of fear can influence a person to behave irrationally. It can be the underlying cause of numerous internal conflicts. For example, if we allow a spirit of fear to guide us, it can affect our self-confidence. We can become fearful about choosing a career, about making career changes, about investing our money, about traveling, or any other common activity.

The goal of a spirit of fear is to make us feel powerless and afraid. It's true that at almost any moment disaster could be lurking around the corner, but if we understand that a spirit of fear is causing us to feel unwarranted concern, we can learn to control it and move forward with determination and poise.

Another spirit, the spirit of envy, can cause a rift in our relationships with family and friends. A spirit of envy encompasses many negative attributes, such as jealousy, greed, spite, covetousness, bitterness, and resentment. A spirit of envy can attach itself to our desires and expectations and manifest itself in how we view ourselves and treat others. It can cause divisions in families, churches, businesses, governments, and any other institution. I will briefly cite a few more of the spirits we encounter on a daily basis, then provide strategies on how to maintain control.

Doubt is another emotion that can be manipulated. The spirit of doubt can cause us to second-guess our decisions. Doubt can undermine our fundamental beliefs and core values, as evidenced in the following case. As you read this case, avoid letting your emotions affect you. It is not cited to arouse your personal convictions. It's cited to challenge you to ask, Is it possible we are not in control of our decisions?

DOUBT

In the early seventies, during an era of hippies, free love, whimsical hopes for peace, opposition to war, and the women's rights movement, a case was presented in court by a woman who alleged she had been raped and who wanted to obtain an abortion. Under the laws of Texas, life was defined as beginning at conception. The only legal reason to perform an abortion in that state was to save a woman's life. But if the litigants could raise enough doubt on when life began, they could change the law. The case proceeded through the court system until it reached the U.S. Supreme Court.

Nine men appointed to the U.S. Supreme Court were faced with rendering one of the most significant decisions of the twentieth century. Their pronouncement is still being hotly debated decades later. The case was *Roe v. Wade* [410 U.S. 113]. Seven U.S. Supreme Court justices voted in favor of Norma McCorvey (a.k.a., Jane Roe), making abortion legal throughout America. Only two justices were opposed to it, even though conservative justices comprised the majority of the Court. This court decision changed the culture of America.

The actions of the *Roe* Court have had staggering ramifications for millions of lives. According to the Catholic Pro-Life Committee's Web site, www.prolifedallas.org, more than fifty million legal abortions have been performed in America since the U.S. Supreme Court delivered its decision on January 22, 1973.[3]

Republican presidents with a desire to overturn the *Roe v. Wade* decision have held office for a total of twenty-three years since this case was decided. Their party held a majority in Congress while at least two of these presidents were in office. They appointed new Supreme Court justices when some of the original members of the *Roe* Court retired. And yet they have not been able to overturn this decision. It is a decision raised during every presidential election. Many Americans cast their vote for president based solely on this issue. For many, it is the single most important issue.

Early in its majority opinion, the U.S. Supreme Court acknowledged, "Our awareness of the sensitive and emotional nature of the abortion controversy, of the vigorous opposing views, even among physicians, and of the deep and seemingly absolute convictions that the subject inspire[s]." They further stated, "Our task, of course, is to resolve the issue by constitutional measurement, free of emotion and of predilection. We seek earnestly to do this."[4]

The justices sought to understand man's attitude toward abortions. They considered the following three reasons, which were presented by the litigants to explain the historical enactment in the nineteenth century of criminal abortion laws in the United States in order to analyze the justification for their continued existence.[5]

The first reason was that "these laws were the product of a Victorian social concern to discourage illicit sexual conduct."[6]

This reason was quickly dismissed by the Court since Texas did not advance this justification and no other court or commentator took this argument seriously.

The second reason was that when most criminal abortion laws were first enacted, the procedure was hazardous for women. The Court concluded that there had been significant medical advances, which mitigated the question of safety, stating "that abortion in early pregnancy, that is, prior to the end of the first trimester, although not without its risk, is now relatively safe. Mortality rates for women undergoing early abortions, where the procedure is legal, appear to be as low as or lower than the rates for normal childbirth."[7]

The third reason was the state's duty to protect prenatal life. The Court reasoned, "Logically, of course, a legitimate state interest in this area need not stand or fall on acceptance of the belief that life begins at conception or at some other point prior to live birth. In assessing the State's interest, recognition may be given to the less rigid claim that as long as at least potential life is involved, the State may assert interests beyond the protection of the pregnant woman alone."[8]

The fundamental question of when life begins became a primary issue in *Roe v. Wade*. The Court concluded that there was sufficient doubt concerning the theory that a new life is present from the moment of conception to leave this question unanswered by saying, "We need not resolve the difficult question of when life begins. When those trained in the respective disciplines of medicine, philosophy, and theology are unable to arrive at any consensus, the judiciary, at this point in the development of man's knowledge, is not in a position to speculate as to the answer."[9]

Deception

For twenty-five years we heard or read about *Roe v Wade* but had very few details about the landmark case. On January 21, 1998, the twenty-fifth anniversary of the case, Norma McCorvey testified under oath before the Senate Subcommittee on the Constitution, Federalism, and Property Rights. During her testimony, she stated that the events in the affidavit she had submitted to the Supreme Court had not happened the way she had said at the time they did. She admitted that she had lied when she said she had been raped.[10]

She said her attorneys, Sarah Weddington and Linda Coffee, "needed an extreme case to make their client look pitiable." She testified that she never intended for her case to be brought before the Supreme Court on behalf of a class of women. She testified, "Sarah and Linda were looking for somebody, anybody, to use to further their own agenda," and that she herself became their "most willing dupe."[11]

In summarizing her testimony before the Senate, Ms. McCorvey stated, "Since all these lies succeeded in dismantling every state's protection of the unborn child, I think it's fair to say that the entire abortion industry is based on a lie."[12]

In 2003, thirty years after the Supreme Court decision legalizing abortion, Ms. McCorvey attempted to reopen the case based on her rights as an original litigant. In *McCorvey v. Hill* [385 F.3d 846], Ms. McCorvey petitioned the U.S. District Court for the Northern District of Texas, Dallas Division to reopen the original *Roe v. Wade* case in light of new evidence that was not available in 1973. The Federal Rule of Civil Procedure 60(b) permits reviews of a court's decision if the request is made within a reasonable time after the judgment. The U.S. District Court for the Northern District of Texas ruled that too much time had elapsed since the original ruling for McCorvey to file her petition. The U.S. Court of Appeals for the Fifth Circuit concurred with the District Court's decision [385 F.3d 846; No. 03-10711]. In 2005, the U.S. Supreme Court denied McCorvey's petition for judicial review, rendering the opinion of the Fifth Circuit Court final.[13]

In her concurrence for the Fifth Circuit Court, Circuit Judge Edith Jones stated:

> Although mootness dictates that Ms. McCorvey has no "live" controversy, the serious and substantial evidence she offered could have generated an important debate over the factual premises that underlay *Roe*....The perverse result of the Court's having determined through constitutional adjudication this fundamental social policy, which affects over a million women and unborn babies each year, is that the facts no longer matter.... The fact that the Court's constitutional decision making leaves our nation in a position of willful blindness to evolving knowledge should trouble any dispassionate observer not only about the abortion decisions, but about a number of other areas in which the Court unhesitatingly steps into the realm of social policy under the guise of constitutional adjudication.[14]

A lie about being raped and the alleged victim's desire to terminate her unwanted pregnancy changed the culture of America. The *Roe* Court's ruling was based on the facts presented. They had no way of knowing the facts were a lie.

Millions of Americans are opposed to abortion, but they have not been able to stop abortions from taking place. When the time came to make one of the most important decisions of their lives, five conservative Supreme Court justices made a choice that was contradictory to their traditional views and fundamental beliefs. Why? What on Earth could have made them do it?

SPIRITUAL INFLUENCES

The *Roe* decision and the circumstances surrounding it serve as a powerful object lesson in the ways in which lies, deception, and doubt can influence judicious, intelligent people to make uncharacteristic decisions that are opposed to their values and beliefs. If enough doubt could be raised concerning the theory that human life is present from the moment of conception, then the devil could prevail in his pursuit to destroy mankind by preventing children from being born. Lies, deception, and doubt are so ingrained in our society that most people do not understand that they come from the devil.

Just as the *Roe* decision is a vivid modern example of how spiritual deception can impact our daily lives, one can also find biblical examples of spiritual influence on people's actions. One example is afforded by the devil's efforts to tempt Jesus to sin.

> Then Jesus was led by the Spirit into the desert to be tempted by the devil. After fasting forty days and forty nights, he was hungry. The tempter came to him and said, "If you are the Son of God, tell these stones to become bread." Jesus answered, "It is written: 'Man does not live on bread alone, but on every word that comes from the mouth of God.'" Then the devil took him to the holy city and had him stand on the highest point of the temple. "If you are the Son of God," he said, "throw yourself down. For it is written: 'He will command his angels concerning you,

and they will lift you up in their hands, so that you will not strike your foot against a stone.'" Jesus answered him, "It is also written: 'Do not put the Lord your God to the test.'" Again, the devil took him to a very high mountain and showed him all the kingdoms of the world and their splendor. "All this I will give you," he said, "if you will bow down and worship me." Jesus said to him, "Away from me, Satan! For it is written: 'Worship the Lord your God, and serve him only.'" Then the devil left him, and angels came and attended him.

—MATTHEW 4:1–11

In this passage, it is clear the devil, also called Satan, is directly trying to influence Jesus to sin. When Scripture speaks of Satan, it is not speaking figuratively. He is real. He is a created being—a fallen angel who rebelled against God. Satan is not God's counterpart. His temptations are real. Satan tempted Jesus in a weak moment when He was hungry. The devil will also try to tempt us in our weakest moments, in areas where we are most vulnerable. It is not sin to be tempted; it is only sin to give in to temptation.

The important context of the devil's temptation of Jesus is what happened just before Jesus went into the wilderness to fast and pray. He was baptized, the heavens opened, and God was "well pleased" with him (Matt. 3:16–17). This shows that Satan will also attack us after a victory, when we are most susceptible to pride. We may become boastful. We may take all the credit for ourselves and not remember the people who helped us succeed. Satan's prideful ambition is the reason he rebelled against God.

PRIMARY CATEGORIES OF TEMPTATION

If we look closely at the three attempts made by the devil to tempt Jesus, they represent three primary categories of temptation: (1) physical needs or desires, (2) power and possessions, and (3) pride or vain self-confidence.

The Bible cautions against making ourselves the top priority in our lives and not caring about others. It tells us, "For all that is in the world, the lust of the flesh, and the lust of the eyes, and the pride of life, is not of the Father, but is of the world" (1 John 2:16, KJV). Another translation states it this way, "For everything in the world—the cravings of sinful man, the lust of his eyes and the boasting of what he has and does—comes not from the Father but from the world" (NIV).

This Scripture depicts the enemy's favorite weapons: First, the lust of the flesh, which is a sinful preoccupation with gratifying one's physical desires. Second, the lust of the eyes, which is a sinful craving to accumulate things to the point where one trusts in the security of one's possessions rather than in God. Third, the pride of life, which is a sinful obsession to achieve status and prestige at all costs with a self-sufficient "I did it all" attitude. Satan tempts us to this day with the three subtle deceptions he tried on Jesus, and he often succeeds. Satan has caused many people to miss out on God's redemptive plan for salvation and the good plans the Lord has for them.

We are all susceptible to influence by supernatural forces during trying experiences or situations involving great emotional investment. During these times, we can subconsciously be influenced to say or do something that causes us to sin. However, just because we are tempted does not mean we have to give in to that temptation. We can follow Jesus' example and not give in.

The Unthinkable

Sometimes people do succumb to temptation and do unthinkable things. Consider the number of horrific stories in the news that attract national attention.

On November 4, 2004, MSNBC reported, "With a calm and dispassionate voice and a hymn playing in the background, Dena Schlosser confessed to the unthinkable, telling a 911 operator she'd cut off the arms of her baby girl."[15] After her first trial ended with a hung jury, she was found not guilty by reason of insanity during her second capital murder trial. Two years after her conviction, in November 2008, CBS-11 TV reported that she had been released from the mental hospital into outpatient treatment because her doctors said she was getting better.[16]

On June 20, 2001, Andrea Yates called 911 and told the operator, "I killed my kids." When the police arrived at her home, they found she had drowned her five children in the bathtub. According to a Court TV report, "Forensic psychiatrist Dr. Phillip Resnick testified that Yates believed Satan had taken over her body and soul and was eyeing her children's souls next." After her original conviction for capital murder was overturned, she was found not guilty by reason of insanity at her second trial.[17]

On February 14, 2008, Steven P. Kazmierczak went to Northern Illinois University and shot twenty-one people, five of them fatally, before killing himself. In a report on CNN.com, university police chief Donald Grady was quoted as saying that Kazmierczak "was someone that was revered by the faculty and staff and students alike." Chief Grady said he been told the killer had been taking medication but "went off his meds a couple of weeks ago."[18]

Based on the very favorable impressions people had of him, what could have caused him to shoot these students and then commit suicide? Is it possible that spiritual forces of evil some-times cause people to become temporarily insane? To shoot other people and then commit suicide?

EVIL PERSONIFIED

When tragedies occur, people often ask, "Why did God do this?" or, "What kind of God would let something like this happen?" In Satan's attempt to separate people from God and keep them from accepting Jesus as their Lord, he deceives people into thinking God is responsible for the evil actions of people. Most people do not consider the possibility that tragedies are caused by Satan and his supernatural demonic forces.

God is never responsible for evil. Satan is. Misguided terror-ists such as those who committed the abominable acts on 9/11 have been brainwashed into believing their actions honor Allah, the supreme being of Islam. Their actions violate the religious teachings and beliefs regarding suicide and murder found in the Koran, the sacred text of Islam. But they have been deceived into killing themselves, along with thousands of innocent victims, under the false pretense that Allah will be pleased with their ac-tions and they will be richly rewarded in paradise.

Jesus warned us there would be those who would be deceived into killing believers, both Jews and Gentiles. In John 16:2–3, Jesus said, "'In fact, a time is coming when anyone who kills you will think he is offering a service to God. They will do such things because they have not known the Father or me.'" Tragically, that time has come. Al Qaeda, the Taliban, and other terrorists have been deceived by Satan to attack and kill the citizens of Chris-tian and Jewish nations.

What on Earth made the terrorists do what they did? Is it pos-sible that these atrocious acts were brought about by supernatural forces of evil? The *Encarta Dictionary* defines *evil* as "the quality of being profoundly immoral or wrong."[19] Other adjectives synonymous with *evil* are *devilish, malicious, wicked, malevolence, sin, iniquity, vice, immoral, foul, vile, nasty, horrible, unpleasant, revolting, disgusting,* and *obnoxious.* These characteristics are the very nature of evil. Satan's nature is evil. He wants dominion over our lives. Satan is evil personified.

Love Never Fails

Just as Satan personifies evil, Jesus personifies love. For a picture of what this means, I can do no better than the apostle Paul's magnificent description of love in 1 Corinthians 13:4–8: "Love is patient, love is kind. It does not envy, it does not boast, it is not proud. It is not rude, it is not self-seeking, it is not easily angered, it keeps no record of wrongs. Love does not delight in evil but rejoices with the truth. It always protects, always trusts, always hopes, always perseveres. Love never fails."

Jesus has already been given dominion over heaven and Earth. Like Jesus, we can use the Word of God to withstand the devil's attacks. We can command him to leave us alone. The Bible tells us, "For God hath not given us the spirit of fear; but of power, and of love, and of a sound mind" (2 Tim. 1:7, KJV). God has given us the power and ability to overcome every spirit; however, that power is useless if we don't believe in the existence of our spiritual opponents. By accepting at least the possibility that there are spiritual forces of evil at work on Earth, we can learn how to recognize them, withstand them, and defeat them. We can become equipped to live successful, victorious lives!

Universal Unconsciousness

*In a world where nothing is what it seems,
you have to look beyond the usual suspects.*

*I*T IS NOT SURPRISING THAT many Christians look to science for explanations regarding human behavior. Some view the concept of the existence of demons as pagan ideology. One reason for their skepticism is that the biblical principle of spiritual warfare is not taught in many churches.

Most Christian denominations are united in their belief in the authority and infallibility of the Bible as God's Word. They agree that the Bible was written by Spirit-inspired writers and that the Word of God is true. But many denominations do not teach their members about spiritual warfare. By remaining silent, or worse, by trying to reconcile their teachings with a naturalistic view of the Bible, they are in effect denying the reality of Satan, demons, and angels. But the Bible teaches, "For our struggle is not against flesh and blood, but against the rulers, against the authorities, against the powers of this dark world and against the spiritual forces of evil in the heavenly realms" (Eph. 6:12). This Scripture clearly tells us that there is an ongoing spiritual war against the powers of darkness. This book seeks to reveal biblical truths concerning the spiritual realities of our struggles. When we deny the actuality of spiritual warfare, we are spurning the Holy Spirit's revelation to us.

A LACK OF KNOWLEDGE

In Hosea 4:6, God warns us, "My people are destroyed from lack of knowledge." Although He was referring to the nation of Israel, this Scripture also applies to us today.

Due to a lack of knowledge, many Christians are missing out on God's plan to be His sanctified ones, set apart to be a light to the world. The devil does not want us to understand the importance of spiritual warfare. He wants us to stay in darkness, ignorant of his plans. So he does everything he can to convince church leaders of every denomination not to teach, preach, or even acknowledge the biblical truth of spiritual warfare.

As a result, many congregations do not understand the effects of spiritual warfare, and they are unaware of how to defend themselves when the attacks come. Many Christian families are devastated by the devil's evil schemes, manifested in ways such as depression, suicide, drug abuse, imprisonment, and job loss due to fighting or stealing or other ungodly behavior. Many marriages have ended in divorce because of adultery, incest, or physical abuse. These are not rare or unusual events; they happen every day due to many factors—unwillingness to forgive, bitterness, anger, lust, and deceit. But imagine the possible outcome of these situations if those involved had been trained prayer warriors equipped to battle the schemes of the devil.

If we want to win, we need to acknowledge the reality of the spiritual war in which we are embroiled, learn the enemy's tactics, and join the winning side.

THE ENEMY'S TACTICS

In his letter to the church at Corinth, the apostle Paul tells us: "The god of this age has blinded the minds of unbelievers, so that they cannot see the light of the gospel of the glory of Christ, who is the image of God" (2 Cor. 4:4). He also says, "We demolish arguments and every pretension that sets itself up against the knowledge of God, and we take captive every thought to make it obedient to Christ" (2 Cor. 10:5). In these Scriptures, the apostle Paul informs us that Satan's plan is to prevent spiritual comprehension from taking place. The devil has blinded people's minds and warped their belief systems and worldviews using false arguments and other pretensions designed to keep them from the knowledge of God.

Deception, doubt, and denial are the main devices used by the devil to separate people from God. He begins his deception by causing people to deny the very existence of God, angels, demons, and the devil himself. I am reminded of a statement by Charles Baudelaire that is quoted in the movie *The Usual Suspects*: "The greatest trick the devil ever pulled was convincing the world he didn't exist."[1] It accurately describes the number one tactic Satan and his demons employ, which is to deceive people into believing they don't exist. They want us to believe that we are in total control of our actions.

Doctrines that reject spiritual explanations of the world and deny God as Creator are an essential ploy of the enemy. One such doctrine, naturalism, prevents many people from accepting even the possibility that spiritual warfare is real. The *Encarta Dictionary* defines *naturalism* as "a system of thought that rejects all spiritual and supernatural explanations of the world and holds that science is the sole basis of what can be known."[2] Another doctrine, Darwinism, advocates the theory of evolution, which provides a wholly natural explanation for the origin of life. This way of thinking opens the door to questioning biblical truths. The devil seeks to replace the truth in our minds and hearts with these and other false doctrines. He wants us to question or doubt God. He creates internal conflict using speculation and lies.

At times, the enemy's tactics may seem so innocent that we don't think to ask ourselves whether we are in control or whether supernatural forces of evil are in fact influencing our decisions. Often, the devil is able to entice people away from God by influencing their friends, family, and other people they trust. Most people who are victims of substance abuse were offered their first alcoholic drink, their first joint of marijuana, or their first line of cocaine by someone they trusted. Most of them never thought they would become addicted. They were deceived into believing it wouldn't happen to them. Once they became addicted, they became open to demonic attacks from a spirit of denial ("I'm not addicted; I only get high on weekends"), a spirit of deception ("I can handle this by myself; no one will ever know"), and a spirit of doubt ("No one can help me; I can't live without it").

Like addictions, compulsions prevent those afflicted by them from being in control of their own behavior. Compulsions create intense internal pressure to satisfy a perceived need. The person is obsessed with behaving a certain way and believes his or her fanatical behavior is justified. Compulsions can open the door for demonic attacks because the compulsive person's focus is generally self-centered.

Some compulsions are related to physical appearance. Society depicts people who are very thin as the ideal of beauty. As a result, many teenagers and adults strive to be skinny. Their self-image becomes bound to the idea that they must remain thin at all costs. A spirit of fear can cause them to have an abhorrence of becoming overweight. Bulimia and anorexia nervosa are eating disorders associated with excessive dieting or anxiety about gaining weight. A person can become so consumed with dieting that it leads to serious health problems, depression, and even death. There is nothing wrong with having the desire to be thin and attractive. Most doctors agree it is healthier to be thin than to be overweight. However, compulsive dieting, like other compulsions, can destroy lives and families.

Although an evil spirit is not associated with everyone who has an eating disorder or exhibits other compulsive behavior, compulsions, like addictions, are doors the enemy can use to launch an attack. In acute cases, the person may need—in addition to receiving treatment from a medical doctor—to consult with a Christian minister gifted in discernment of evil spirits in order to receive complete deliverance.

Thankfully, God has given us weapons to overcome any and all of the enemy's attacks. We do not have to face the enemy unarmed, on his terms, or wielding his weapons. God has equipped us with spiritual weapons and spiritual gifts. He has given His angels charge over us, and He has sent His Holy Spirit to protect us. After citing a few further illustrations of the enemy's tactics, we will cover winning strategies for taking a stand against spiritual forces of evil and utilizing the powerful resources God has given us so that we may prevail over the enemy.

WAYS THAT SEEM RIGHT TO MAN

In Proverbs 16:25, we find a warning about the costly consequences of subtle deceptions: "There is a way that seems right to a man, but in the end it leads to death." In this scripture, the word *death* is taken from the Hebrew word *maveth*, which in *Strong's Concordance* is given both a literal meaning, "to die," and the figurative meanings of "ruin" and "spiritual death."[3]

Compulsions and addictions are examples of subtle deceptions whose consequences cost their sufferers dearly in a literal sense. An example of how the enemy's deceptions can lead to spiritual death can be found in the attitude of some churches toward Halloween.

Even though Halloween has traditionally been associated

with evil, the devil, witches, and demons, many churches across the nation host "harvest" events on October 31. Although they claim not to be celebrating Halloween, what subtle message are they sending to the thousands of non-Christians who drive past their churches every day and see pumpkins for sale on church property and signs advertising their October 31 activities? Although the children who attend these events are encouraged to wear costumes that are not scary and that do not promote ungodly principles, what do passersby think when they see children dressed in costumes on October 31 going to church and leaving with bags of candy?

In Mark 11:15–16, we read how Jesus zealously maintained the sanctity of the house of God and of the area surrounding it. He drove out the people who were buying and selling in the temple and would not allow anyone to carry merchandise through the temple courts. In Mark 11:17, Jesus says, "'Is it not written: "My house will be called a house of prayer for all nations"? but you have made it "a den of robbers."'" We read in Colossians 4:5, "Be wise in the way you act toward outsiders; make the most of the opportunity." The church has a responsibility to let Christ's light shine so the outside world will be drawn to Him.

To some people, it may seem OK for churches to host events on Halloween. Many Christians say, "We don't celebrate Halloween, but we want to provide a fun, safe environment for our children that night." Some even believe it's an acceptable form of outreach. However, the church has many other ways in which it can reach out to the community and share the good news of Christ without hosting Halloween events.

Why do churches feel compelled to host activities on Halloween? Is it possible that supernatural forces of evil have penetrated our churches and deceived our church leaders? Could a spirit of denial—"We don't celebrate Halloween"—be at work? Or a spirit of deception—"It's OK to wear costumes that don't promote ungodly principles"? Or a spirit of doubt—"I don't think that passersby will be negatively influenced by our church hosting an event on Halloween."

The autumn is a beautiful time of year to celebrate the bountiful blessings of the Lord. God enjoys celebrations, fellowship, and praise. Many churches host fall festivals on other dates to express their thankfulness and bring glory to God.

FOR YOUR OWN GOOD

Another tactic Satan uses is to present an idea as a benefit for our own good. For example, in 2005, at many churches across the nation, the decision was made to close on Christmas Day since it was a Sunday. These church leaders apparently believed their congregations would rather spend Christmas with their families than attend church. Regular church members and visitors seeking to attend church on Christmas were forced to try to find another place to worship and celebrate the birth of our Lord and Savior, Jesus Christ.

What could influence church leaders to close their doors on Christmas yet be open on Halloween? Is it possible that these ways that seem right to man are the result of spiritual warfare?

KEEP THE ENEMY OUT!

Churches that host activities on Halloween may be opening themselves up to the influence of the devil by attracting people who practice witchcraft. Some may consider this fanatical thinking because *witchcraft* is a term that they reject. Many people don't believe that witches exist. However, there really are people in this world who worship Satan and practice witchcraft. There is a large group of witches, the Wiccans, in the United States. The founders of Wicca in the United States are Gavin and Yvonne Frost. The following excerpt was taken from the Web site of The Church and School of Wicca.

> When a shared interest in the occult and in alternative spiritual paths brought them together, they moved to St. Louis, Missouri, where they founded the Church and School of Wicca in 1968. At that time they started an occult correspondence school teaching Witchcraft as a spiritual path, along with astral travel, sorcery, astrology, and psychic healing through the mails to a worldwide student body. With the publication of *The Witch's Bible* and later *The Magic Power of Witchcraft*, the student body grew. They taught thousands of students the fundamentals of their spiritual philosophy.
>
> Eventually the Church developed branch covens and churches across the United States. Although officially the Frosts are semi-retired, they continue to write books and to lecture at various pagan gatherings around the nation. Each year at Hallowe'en they can guarantee dozens of radio interviews and several TV appearances. This furthers the general population's interest in Wicca and de-demonizes it.
>
> They have always been cutting-edge philosophers and have made no bones about sexual activity within covens. Their candor has alienated many "plastic" pagans and caused the Frosts to be controversial within the new-age metaphysical subculture. That controversy itself has generated many students coming to criticize

who are then surprisingly convinced by what we teach.[4]

Witchcraft is real. Churches that host activities on Halloween may be contributing to "de-demonizing" it. They may also unintentionally be furthering the general population's interest in witchcraft and the occult.

Everything Is Not What It Seems

Satan worship is not limited to witchcraft and covens. It is also manifested in other forms of occult practices, such as psychic hotlines, voodoo, fortune telling, horoscopes, palm reading, and holding séances.

Occult practices have begun to proliferate in our society, especially on television (both cable and network stations) and over the Internet. Television programs such as *Sabrina the Teenage Witch, Charmed,* and *The Wizards of Waverly Place* and movies such as *Practical Magic* and the popular *Harry Potter* series, as well as books of this kind, have made witchcraft seem acceptable and harmless.

Our worldly wisdom says, "Live and let live," "It's not my concern," "There's nothing wrong with this," "It's harmless." That is exactly what Satan wants us to think. When the *Harry Potter* books became popular, some Christians were criticized for refusing to allow their children to read them. What these critics didn't understand is that by reading these books, children could be deceived into believing there is nothing wrong with witchcraft or the occult. But God hates witchcraft and all forms of the occult. Deuteronomy 18:9–12 says, "Thou shalt not learn to do after the abominations of those nations. There shall not be found among you any one...that useth divination, or an observer of times, or an enchanter, or a witch. Or a charmer, or a consulter with familiar spirits, or a wizard, or a necromancer. For all that do these things are an abomination unto the LORD" (KJV).

You may not agree that witchcraft is real or that it is harmful to permit your children to be exposed to it. You may have been deceived into believing the Old Testament does not have any relevance today. However, God is warning us in this passage to protect ourselves from Satan's evil devices, which are meant to harm us and our families.

NEW AGE SPIRITUALITY

In the 1960s, the New Age movement began to take hold, and it has become increasingly popular. According to consultants at Religious Tolerance, a number of fundamental beliefs are held by many New Age followers. One belief, pantheism, is defined on their Web site as "the concept of the divinity of the individual, that we are all gods. [Pantheists] do not seek God as revealed in a sacred text or [as existing] in a remote heaven; they seek God within the self and throughout the entire universe."[5] *The American Heritage College Dictionary* defines *pantheism* as "[a] doctrine identifying Deity with all the universe and its phenomena; belief in and worship of all gods."[6]

According to the section on Religious Tolerance's Web site titled "New Age Beliefs," New Age followers possess a variety of fundamental beliefs, though adherents are encouraged to "shop" for the tenants and practices that best suit them. One of those beliefs is personal transformation, which according this Web site is:

> A profoundly intense mystical experience [that] will lead to the acceptance and use of New Age beliefs and practices. Guided imagery, hypnosis, meditation, and (sometimes) the use of hallucinogenic drugs are useful to bring about and

enhance this transformation. Believers hope to develop new potentials within themselves: the ability to heal oneself and others, psychic powers, a new understanding of the workings of the universe, etc. Later, when sufficient numbers of people have achieved these powers, a major spiritual, physical, psychological and cultural planet-wide transformation is expected.[7]

Some practices of New Age followers are as follows: meditating to release oneself from conscious thinking; divination to foretell the future; astrology to predict a person's future and personality; and holistic health practices, which attempt to cure disorders in mind, body, and spirit and to promote wholeness and balance in the individual. The latter is accomplished using techniques such as crystal healing, meditation, and psychic healing.

Some practitioners attempt to make contact with the spirit world through channeling. Channeling is a method similar to that used by spiritists to summon the spirit of a dead person. There are many reasons people attempt to conjure up spirits. Some do it out of curiosity; others try to contact someone they knew but who is now deceased, and still others do it to gain power or to gratify selfish desires (both good and evil). Seeking this kind of spiritual experience can open the door to deception and manipulation by demons.

Yoga is a common form of meditation that many people practice without understanding its origin and meaning. According to Wikipedia:

Yoga refers to traditional physical and mental disciplines originating in India. The word is associated with meditative practices in Buddhism and Hinduism. The Sanskrit word yoga is derived from the Sanskrit root *yuj,* meaning "to control," "to yoke," or "to unite." Raja yoga is a system for control of the mind. Hatha yoga focuses on the purification of the physical body, leading to the purification of the mind. Zen Buddhism is often set alongside yoga. In 1989, the Vatican declared that Eastern meditation practices such as Zen and yoga can "degenerate into a cult of the body."[8]

New Age spirituality, Zen Buddhism, channeling, transcendental meditation, and yoga are all deceptive devices designed to create a state of being that separates the practitioner from trusting and believing in God and accepting His Son, Jesus, as Lord.

The Reality of Demonization

Dr. Ed Murphy, a respected Christian leader, scholar, and author of *The Handbook for Spiritual Warfare,* wrote in the introduction to his book about a real-life experience he and his family had with the occult. In the 1960s, his fourteen-year-old daughter, Carolyn, unwittingly became involved in the occult by wearing a necklace with what she described as a good-luck charm that all the kids were wearing. It turned out to be a pentagram, which is a symbol of the occult world. Her boyfriend had given her the necklace. He also introduced her to demonic heavy rock music and transcendental meditation.[9]

Dr. Murphy said evil spirits changed his daughter's sweet personality into an evil, rebellious attitude. He saw the demons glaring through her eyes and heard her tearful pleas for help. Carolyn and her father prayed fervent prayers for her deliverance in the name and authority of Jesus. Her deliverance was successful only after she confessed her rebellious attitude; completely renounced her involvement in the occult; and destroyed the symbols of that way of life, including the necklace, the charms, the heavy rock music albums, and everything she had in her possession that dishonored God.[10]

Carolyn's experience is just one example among many documented instances of demonization found in Dr. Murphy's books. If you have a hard time believing that witchcraft and the occult are real, the enemy may be influencing your thoughts—telling you that these things must not exist because you have never experienced them for yourself.

Dr. Charles Kraft, a professor of anthropology and intercultural communication at Fuller Theological Seminary in Pasadena, California, and author of the book *Defeating Dark Angels,* wrote about the myth that demonization (demonic oppression or demonic attachment in a person's life) is uncommon in the United States:

> First, they assume that the Christian influence in America has been sufficient to thwart demonization. Second, they assume that demonization will be obvious. Third, based on that assumption, they further assume that demonic activity occurs only where it is obvious, such as in other societies. This common myth is extremely damaging. The Enemy is delighted to see so many Christian leaders, churches, and believers buy into this lie.[11]

Dr. Kraft provides a good description of the universal unconsciousness that exists regarding demons in the United States. He has ministered to many people oppressed by demons. He primarily treats Christians, so his personal involvement has been mostly with demon-oppressed people rather than demon-possessed people. His book details numerous encounters with demons and his success in setting people free from their bondage.

Denial and unbelief are tools used by the devil to keep the

biblical principle of spiritual warfare from being taught in many churches. If the devil can perpetuate the myth that demonization is not real or that it's very rare, then people won't seek the help they need to break free from demonic oppression in their lives.

The Bible makes it clear that demons exist. There are numerous accounts in Scripture of Jesus and His disciples commanding them to leave the people they possess. In the Gospel of Matthew, we are told, "Many who were demon-possessed were brought to him, and he drove out the spirits with a word" (Matt. 8:16).

In the Gospel of Mark, more than half of Jesus' recorded ministry involves setting people free from demons. In the first chapter, a man in the synagogue possessed by an evil spirit is set free (Mark 1:23–26). This is biblical support that even a churchgoer can have an evil spirit. In Mark 9:14–27, we read of a demon-possessed child. Demons will also attack our children.

In the Gospel of Luke, by Jesus' authority, "demons came out of many people" and "those troubled by evil spirits were cured" (Luke 4:41; 6:18). He gave His disciples power to drive out all demons (Luke 9:1).

In the Gospel of John, Jesus is accused of being demon-possessed (John 8:48–52), and Satan enters one of the disciples (John 13:27).

The evil spirits of whom we find evidence throughout the Bible did not cease to exist after the Bible was written. Demons are real. Demonization is real. In his book *Defeating Dark Angels*, Dr. Kraft lists activities that he believes demonic forces carry out in the everyday lives of Christians and non-Christians alike.

> Demons are involved in every kind of disruption....They tempt and entice to get people to make bad or at least unwise decisions. And when they find someone already in difficulty, they work to make it worse.

Demons apparently can put thoughts in our minds, though, again, we are responsible for what we do with those thoughts. Since demons know what each of us is susceptible to, they will tailor the thoughts they put in our minds.

Demons seek to keep people ignorant of their presence and activities. Demons love it when people don't believe they exist....Demons delight in working behind the scenes, pushing people to react in dysfunctional ways and then encouraging them to blame themselves...and making them think they are psychological problems!

Another demonic tactic is to get people to fear them. If they can't keep people ignorant, often their next strategy is to work on people's fears of what they don't understand or what they see as potentially embarrassing....When one realizes how little power the enemy has compared to that of God, very little fear should remain.

In all satanic activity, deceit is a major weapon....A favorite trick: deluding people that false ideas are their own (usually negative thinking about themselves, others and God).

Demons try to keep people from God or from doing anything God wants. They hinder unbelievers from believing (2 Corinthians 4:4). They also work to undermine the faith of Christians.

Demons, like Satan, are accusers....A common tactic is to convince people to accuse themselves, others and God of causing whatever may be undermining their health, life, love, relationships and anything else....Demons encourage rumors, cultivate misunderstandings, and justify anger at and blame of God.

Demons reinforce compulsions. Demons delight in helping people develop compulsions toward both good and bad behavior. Demons reinforce such compulsions as lust, drugs, alcohol, tobacco, overeating, undereating, pornography, gambling, materialism, competitiveness....They also encourage exaggerated attention to many things ordinarily considered "good." Among such compulsions are work, study, attractive dress, religion, family, achievement, and success.

Harassment: another demonic tool. A major concern is to disrupt people's lives...through influencing such things as health, relationships, worship, sleep, diet, and machines (especially cars and computers).[12]

Each of the above activities is meant to draw us in one way or another into sin or out of step with God's plan for our lives. According to Dr. Kraft, demons do attempt to influence our day-to-day lives. However, demons are not the cause of all bad things that happen in our lives. The law of cause and effect still plays a major role. And though demonic forces try to disrupt our lives, we can learn how to defeat them and take control.

WAYS TO BRING DOWN DEMONIC FORCES

There are several things that we can do to bring down demonic forces.

First and foremost is to accept Jesus Christ as your Lord and Savior. This not only secures God's redemptive plan for you but also delivers a deadly blow to Satan, because he can no longer claim you for his kingdom of darkness. It also adds another soldier to God's army who can bring more people to Christ, as Jesus commanded His disciples to do: "Therefore go and make disciples of all nations, baptizing them in the name of the Father and of the Son and of the Holy Spirit, and teaching them to obey everything I have commanded you" (Matt. 28:19–20).

Reach out to God with fervent prayer and praise. "Sing to the LORD, praise his name; proclaim his salvation day after day. Declare his glory among the nations, his marvelous deeds among all peoples. For great is the LORD and most worthy of praise" (Ps. 96:2–4).

Renew your mind. Break old cycles in your thinking process. Carefully consider whether your plans represent godly wisdom or worldly wisdom before taking action. "You were taught, with regard to your former way of life, to put off your old self, which is being corrupted by its deceitful desires; to be made new in the attitude of your minds; and to put on the new self, created to be like God in true righteousness and holiness" (Eph. 4:22–24).

Study God's Word so you can know the difference between godly wisdom and worldly wisdom. "Your word is a lamp to my feet and a light for my path" (Ps. 119:105).

Trust God completely by seeking His advice in all matters in your life. "Trust in the LORD with all your heart and lean not on your own understanding; in all your ways acknowledge him, and he will make your paths straight" (Prov. 3:5–6).

"Fight the good fight of the faith" (1 Tim. 6:12). This means to believe and act on God's Word, for we should "be doers of the word, and not hearers only" (James 1:22, NKJV). Take a stand for what is right, even when others mock you or question your beliefs.

And finally, love others as Jesus loves you (John 15:12).

LIVE IN VICTORY

We do not have to live defeated lives. Our most powerful weapon against the enemy is the authority we have in Jesus as born-again believers. Jesus defeated the devil and his demons when He bore all our iniquities, grief, sorrows, and sicknesses on the cross; He died and overcame death in His resurrection from the dead. We can choose to exercise the authority we have through Jesus and live in victory.

If you have not accepted Christ Jesus as Lord and Savior of your life, then I invite you to pray the following prayer:

> *Heavenly Father, it is written in Your Holy Word that if I confess with my mouth that Jesus is Lord and believe in my heart that You raised Jesus from the dead, then I shall be saved. Father, I confess that Jesus is my Lord. I make Him Lord of my life right now. I believe in my heart that You raised Your Son, Jesus, from the dead. I renounce my past life with Satan and close the door to all his devices. I thank You for forgiving me of all my sins and for saving me. Jesus is my Lord! In the name of Jesus I pray, amen.*

The enemy will not cease and desist from his attacks just because you have become a Christian. However, accepting Jesus as your Lord and Savior and placing your faith and trust in Him guarantees your victory. Through Jesus, we can be certain of winning in our daily battles and can live victorious lives. God will give us the power, insight, and confidence to defeat the enemy and claim the victory.

The Invisible Behind the Visible

Do you look at things according to the outward appearance?

2 Corinthians 10:7, NKJV

*E*VERY ONE OF US IS at war with Satan and subject to his attacks. The war is over the control of our life. We are each living beings who have a body, spirit, and soul. *The American Heritage College Dictionary* defines *spirit* as follows: "The part of a human associated with the mind, will and feelings." And *soul* is defined as "the animating and vital principle in human beings, credited with the faculties of thought, action, and emotion and often conceived as an immaterial entity."[1] Spiritual warfare begins in our mind, which controls our thoughts, perceptions, imagination, will, and emotions.

Some people have already conceded defeat because they believe that what will be, will be. They have surrendered the control over their lives to fate. In Greek and Roman mythology, the Fates were the three goddesses (demons) who were said to control human destiny. Fate often leads to an unfavorable destiny or doom. Fatalism, the doctrine expressed in this attitude, views all events as predetermined and unalterable. This dispensationalist view is still taught in many churches. People are taught that God's will is being done in this present dispensation. In other words, God approves of everything that happens, and because

God is sovereign, everything that happens is God's will. This assumption is now changing in many churches. According to Dr. C. Peter Wagner, "God is absolutely sovereign, but Satan is active. Satan acts forcefully against the will of God. Some things in life are caused by Satan. That's the way our Sovereign God has arranged this world. God does not want people to be poor, at war, oppressed, demonized, sick or lost."[2]

A fatalist mentality will not overthrow the enemy or enable anyone to take control of situations that arise in life. It can be compared to a slave mentality that subjects the person to a life of bondage. This is actually one of Satan's tricks to subdue us into thinking that everything we do is hopeless. But there is always hope. Faith, as Hebrews 11:1 says, "is being sure of what we hope for and certain of what we do not see." Faith changes things. Through faith in Jesus, we will realize that the chains of bondage have been broken. Through faith, we will develop spiritual eyes to see the invisible behind the visible and take control of our lives. Jesus came so we could have a more abundant life and have it now (John 10:10)!

Christians are provided with supernatural support in their struggle against the enemy: "For though we live in the world, we do not wage war as the world does" (2 Cor. 10:3). Even though we are fighting this war in the earthly realm, our war is a spiritual one and "the weapons we fight with are not the weapons of the world" (2 Cor. 10:4). These weapons are powerful and able to defeat the enemy in every circumstance. They are discussed in detail in the next chapter, but first it may be helpful to describe what a demonic attack looks like in the natural realm.

Warring Against Demonic Attacks

Many people try to be good and honest and to do what is right. But they try to do it in their own strength without God. The devil can use this self-reliance as an entrance into their lives. Demonic influences can be manifested as pride, anger, bitterness, resentment, rebellion, fear, guilt, worry, criticism, depression, or doubt. They can also be manifested in compulsions, such as an obsessive desire to control and dominate, or in addictions, such as drugs, alcohol, or gambling.

We are all susceptible to temptation in these areas, but we will not all give in to the temptation. The presence of any of these emotions, compulsions, or addictions does not always indicate demonic involvement. However, any one of them could open us up to a demonic attack.

Pride is often used by Satan to convince people they are self-sufficient and don't need God. The spirit of pride will whisper lies such as, "You can do this yourself," "You don't need God," and "Why bother God with this situation? You're smart enough to handle this yourself." When the devil tempts you to "do it yourself," remind yourself that he is not your friend and that he does not want you to succeed.

Sometimes when people are betrayed by a loved one and allow a spirit of unforgiveness to take hold, they can become subject to multiple attacks from other evil spirits, such as the spirits of anger, bitterness, and depression. In extreme cases, the spirit of murder or the spirit of suicide may try to influence them to violently take matters into their own hands.

We are instructed in Ephesians 4 "to put off [our] old self, which is being corrupted by its deceitful desires; to be made new in the attitude of [our] minds" (Eph. 4:22–23). And also, "Do not let the sun go down while you are still angry, and do not give the devil a foothold" (Eph. 4:26–27). These Scriptures alert us to the importance of controlling our minds and our emotions. Failing to do so can open the door to the devil, giving him access into our lives.

Ephesians 4 concludes by telling us to speak words that encourage others; to not grieve the Holy Spirit; and to get rid of all bitterness, rage, anger, brawling, slander, and every form of malice. We are to be kind and compassionate to one another, forgiving each other, just as in Christ God forgave us (Eph. 4:29–32). Changing our way of thinking and the way we respond to life's temptations and challenges will reduce our susceptibility to demonic attacks.

Another way to thwart the enemy's attacks is to abide in God's Word. Jesus told us, "If you remain in me and my words remain in you, ask whatever you wish, and it will be given you" (John 15:7). We are assured in this verse that as long as we feed our minds and spirits with God's Word and align ourselves with Jesus, we can ask Him for help in times of trouble and He will answer us. To abide in the Word means to study God's Word seriously, apply God's Word faithfully, and teach others what we have learned so that they may apply it to their own lives.

Spiritual warfare is not confined to individuals; demonic attacks have created global strongholds throughout the world. In many regions of the earth, the devil attacks the populace by controlling their spiritual atmosphere. Global demonic strongholds are evident by the presence of antichrist systems, such as those in the Middle East, India, and China.

Warring with an Antichrist System

In *The Future War of the Church,* Dr. Chuck Pierce provides a scholarly, in-depth look at spiritual warfare. While my goal is merely to open your eyes to accept the possibility of spiritual warfare, Dr. Pierce's goal is to fully equip you for battle.

In his book, Dr. Pierce relates a prophecy given to him by God on October 27, 2000. In this prophecy, the Lord told him, "You are warring with an antichrist system. Therefore, do not fear this supernatural war that I am calling My people to be engaged in."[3] God has called us into battle, but we are not to be afraid of the demonic structures—antichrist systems—we are warring against.

The prefix *anti-* is defined in *The American Heritage College Dictionary* as "a person who is opposed to a group; opposition to; against."[4] The word *Antichrist* can be interpreted to mean anything or anyone that is opposed to Christ or Christians, or is working against them.[5] The word *system* has many meanings in the same dictionary; the definition that seems best to describe the term as used in *an antichrist system* is: "a set of interrelated ideas or principles; a social, economic or political organizational form."[6]

An antichrist system can be interpreted to mean any doctrine; system of religion, policy, belief; social or political organization; set of principles or laws; or economic structure that systematically opposes Christ or the teaching of Christ.

THE SPIRIT OF ANTICHRIST

The apostle John wrote about the spirit of antichrist in the epistles. In 1 John chapter 2, he wrote to the Christian church to help them understand the internal struggles they were having against the devil, which were caused in part by the false teachings of "many antichrists" (1 John 2:18). The Roman world and many of the Jewish leaders had a philosophical mind-set that was anti-Christ. They were fundamentally opposed to the ideas, beliefs, and behaviors of Christians. They rejected the truth that Jesus is the Son of God.

So the apostle John warned his readers about "antichrists" and the Antichrist, who would try to lead them away from the truth (1 John 2:18–29). He told them how to discern whether teachings were false.

> Dear friends, do not believe every spirit, but test
> the spirits to see whether they are from God,
> because many false prophets have gone out into
> the world. This is how you can recognize the
> Spirit of God: Every spirit that acknowledges
> that Jesus Christ has come in the flesh is from
> God, but every spirit that does not acknowledge
> Jesus is not from God. This is the spirit of the
> antichrist, which you have heard is coming and
> even now is already in the world.
>
> —1 John 4:1–3

The spirit of antichrist denies both the incarnation of Christ and His divine nature. In the apostle John's time, there were many antichrists, such as the Roman emperor, the Gnostics, the Nicolaitans, the Sadducees, the Pharisees, and many of the other Jewish leaders.

Today, many Antichrists have infiltrated our churches. They preach messages of complacency and conformity, and, similar to the Pharisees and Sadducees, they seek the approval of the world rather than the approval of God. And again like the religious leaders who interfered with Jesus' earthly ministry, modern Antichrists mislead many people from the truth of the gospel of Christ.

Certain antichrist religions, such as Hinduism, Buddhism, and Islam, are very powerful because they control the politics, religion, governments, and economies of billions of people. In many countries—Afghanistan, India, Indonesia, Pakistan, Somalia, and Saudi Arabia, among them—proselytizing for Christ is a criminal act. Other countries such as India that do allow the gospel to be preached nevertheless permit existing Christians to practice their faith only under severe restrictions. They do not permit Christians to try to convert others to Christ, and they respond harshly to allegations of forced conversions.

Despite India being the world's largest democracy, with a population of over 1.1 billion people, Christians there face mounting pressure and persecution, particularly from extremist Hindu nationalists. In 2008, according to *Christianity Today*, violence against Christians in Orissa led to murder, physical abuse, and the destruction of over 150 churches and 300 villages.[7] Globally, persecution has increased. Christians are suffering for their faith in countries as widespread as Iran and Burma, North Korea and Saudi Arabia, Vietnam and Colombia.[8]

In a news report on September 10, 2008, from New Delhi, India, *Compass Direct News* reported:

> Tensions continued in the eastern state of Orissa, Hindu nationalist groups intensified attacks on churches and Christian institutions in the southern state of Karnataka. Sajan K. George of the Global Council of Indian Christians (GCIC) told Compass that a mob of more than 200 people attacked the Mission Action Prayer Fellowship church in Bada village of Davangere district on Sunday [September 7, 2008], accusing the Christians of "forcible" conversions. The attack took place during the worship service. Besides assaulting believers and the pastor, the mob burned the Bibles, musical instruments and furniture in front of the church.[9]

One thing Christians can do to take a stand in the battle against these antichrist systems is to pray for the Christians suffering oppression in foreign countries. Pray that the laws of these countries will be changed so that the good news of the gospel of Christ can be freely preached everywhere. And pray that the citizens of these countries will become free to convert to Christianity without reprisals and persecution.

THE SOURCE OF THE INTERNAL SPIRITUAL BATTLE

In Genesis 3:15, God tells the devil (in the form of the serpent that deceived Eve), "I will put enmity between you and the woman, and between your offspring and hers." *Enmity* is defined in *The American Heritage College Dictionary* as "deep hatred or hostility, as between enemies or opponents."[10] In this passage, God describes the profound hatred the devil and his offspring have for mankind. God lets us know that the devil is our enemy.

In John 8:44, Jesus confirms this by saying, "You belong to your father, the devil, and you want to carry out your father's desire. He was a murderer from the beginning, not holding to the truth, for there is no truth in him. When he lies, he speaks his native language, for he is a liar and the father of lies." Jesus asks why His accusers do not believe in Him, then concludes by saying, "He who belongs to God hears what God says. The reason you do not hear is that you do not belong to God" (v. 47). God's children hear and believe what God says. Satan's children do not listen to God. They listen to their father, the father of lies.

Paul communicates the same message in Ephesians 2:2–3, writing that non-believers walk "according to the course of this world, according to the prince of the power of the air, of the spirit that is now working in the sons of disobedience...indulging the desires of the flesh and of the mind...by nature children of wrath" (NASB). This Scripture describes the source of the internal spiritual battle that leads to ungodly choices by the "children of wrath." The source is the prince of the power of the air, the spirit of the devil. The Holy Spirit abides in Christians, but the devil is "working in the sons of disobedience." In *Strong's Concordance*, the Greek word for "disobedience" is *apeithes*. The definition for *apeithes* is "disbelief (obstinate and rebellious), disobedience, unbelief."[11]

In 1 John 3, we are told that the children of the devil do not practice righteousness; they practice sin and hate their brethren. The devil and his offspring are continually plotting against mankind. They are our enemy. They are enemies of the kingdom of God.

Understanding the Enemy

Now that we have identified our enemy, we need to try to understand his character, his strategies, and his methods of attack so that we can equip ourselves with the weapons necessary to defeat him.

The apostle Peter tells us, "Your enemy the devil prowls around like a roaring lion looking for someone to devour" (1 Pet. 5:8). The lion is often referred to as the king of the jungle. Because of its superiority over the other animals in its domain, the lion has the ability to slay anything in its kingdom without fear. It will forcefully seek to take new territory. It will roam the open fields laying claim to everything in its path. It will not stop. It will not back down.

Like a roaring lion, the devil is continually seeking whom he may devour, both Christians and non-Christians alike. He hates all mankind. The devil will not ignore you. If he can catch you, he will fight to keep you in his power. He will not willingly let you go.

However, the devil is not omnipresent. He can only be in one place at a time, which is why he uses his demons to attack us. Nor are Satan and his demons all-powerful. They cannot make something out of nothing; they can only magnify and distort something that is already there. For example, fear—if a person is fearful, then the spirit of fear can use that emotion to torment him or her. If a person has an unnatural desire for sex, then the spirit of lust can use that person's desire to influence them to crave pornography, to become a pedophile, to commit incest, or to participate in other forms of unnatural sex. A spirit of greed may cause a person to wrongfully obtain wealth. These are only three examples of the many evil spirits who manifest on Earth and the methods they use to attack us.

Demons are fallen angels who joined Satan in his attempt to overthrow God. They were not strong enough to defeat their Creator, the almighty God. They lost the battle and were hurled out of heaven (Rev. 12:9). Demons know, just like the devil, that they are destined for the lake of fire and brimstone (Matt. 25:41). These angry evil spirits want to try to convince mankind to join in their rebellion against God and join them in hell.

God loves us and has given us everything we need to prevail against demonic attacks. He has given us His beloved Son Jesus to save us. He has given us his Holy Spirit to comfort us. He has given His angels charge over us to protect us. And He has provided us with spiritual gifts and armed us with spiritual weapons to overcome the enemy. Praise God, we have the power to overcome!

THE HIDDEN AGENDA

In the Book of Matthew, Jesus asks His disciples, "Who do people say the Son of Man is?" (Matt. 16:13). They answer with the names of various prophets, such as Elijah and Jeremiah. But when Jesus asks them, "Who do you say I am?" Simon Peter responds, "You are the Christ, the Son of the living God" (vv. 15–16). Jesus responds by prophesying to Peter, "Blessed are you, Simon son of Jonah, for this was not revealed to you by man, but by my Father in heaven. And I tell you that you are Peter, and on this rock I will build my church, and the gates of Hades will not overcome it. I will give you the keys of the kingdom of heaven; whatever you bind on earth will be bound in heaven, and whatever you loose on earth will be loosed in heaven" (vv. 17–19).

Shortly after prophesying this, Jesus tells His disciples that He needs to go to Jerusalem and that He will be killed and on the third day raised to life again. Peter takes Jesus aside and rebukes Him, saying, "Never, Lord! This shall never happen to you" (Matt. 16:22). Jesus responds, "Get behind me, Satan! You are a stumbling block to me; you do not have in mind the things of God, but the things of men" (v. 23).

Jesus understood the invisible behind the visible. He knew that in this moment Satan was speaking through Peter. Therefore, He rebuked Peter for aligning himself with Satan's plan to deter Him from fulfilling His mission.

In the footnotes to these passages in the *Life Application Study Bible,* we find the following:

> Peter, Jesus' friend and devoted follower who had just eloquently proclaimed Jesus' true identity, sought to protect him from the suffering he prophesied. But if Jesus hadn't suffered and died, Peter (and we) would have died in his sins. Great temptations can come from those who love us and seek to protect us. Be cautious of advice from a friend who says, "Surely God doesn't want you to face this." Often our most difficult temptations come from those who are only trying to protect us from discomfort. In his desert temptations, Jesus heard the message that he could achieve greatness without dying (Matt. 4:6). Here he heard the same message from Peter. Peter had just recognized Jesus as Messiah; here,

however, he forsook God's perspective and evaluated the situation from a human one. Satan is always trying to get us to leave God out of the picture. Jesus rebuked Peter for this attitude.[12]

How quickly and unknowingly we can be influenced by the devil to do something that is harmful, even when our intentions are to do something good. Peter rebuked Jesus out of what he believed was love and concern. However, Satan was influencing Peter's thinking without the disciple's knowledge.

WE ARE NOT ALONE

Fortunately, we have an intercessor: Jesus. He loves His flock and watches over them and protects them from the enemy. In John 10:11–16, Jesus tells us:

> I am the good shepherd. The good shepherd lays down his life for the sheep. The hired hand is not the shepherd who owns the sheep. So when he sees the wolf coming, he abandons the sheep and runs away. Then the wolf attacks the flock and scatters it. The man runs away because he is a hired hand and cares nothing for the sheep. I am the good shepherd; I know my sheep and my sheep know me—just as the Father knows me and I know the Father—and I lay down my life for the sheep. I have other sheep that are not of this sheep pen. I must bring them also. They too will listen to my voice, and there shall be one flock and one shepherd.

After Jesus spoke these words, the people who heard Him attributed His teachings to demons. The Bible tells us in John 10:19–21, "At these words the Jews were again divided. Many of them said, 'He is demon-possessed and raving mad. Why listen to him?' But others said, 'These are not the sayings of a man possessed by a demon. Can a demon open the eyes of the blind?'" People on both sides of the argument acknowledged the existence of demons and the influence they have in the natural realm. However, they lacked discernment concerning Satan's use of deception to create controversy in order to prevent them from knowing the truth about Jesus.

Jesus, the Son of God, was in their midst, yet they were blinded to the truth of His nature. Instead of asking, "Can a demon open the eyes of the blind?" they should have asked, "Can a demon blind the eyes of someone who can see?"

During battles in the natural realm, soldiers sometimes use cunning, lies, and deceit to defeat their enemy. Satan employs the same tactics in the spiritual realm. He plants seeds of doubt to keep people from accepting the truth that Jesus cares about us and wants to protect us from him and his demons.

Jesus knows what Satan is and is never fooled by him. In Matthew 4, Satan comes to Jesus after Jesus has been fasting for forty days and forty nights. He tries to tempt Jesus to sin in order to stop God's plan for our salvation. Jesus permits Satan to take Him to a high place from which they can see all the kingdoms of the earth. But Jesus never loses sight of what Satan is or of the Father's purpose for His life, death, and resurrection.

Eternal Victory

As Christians, the Holy Spirit abides in us and guides us. By listening to His quiet, inner voice, we can learn to discern between the voice of the devil and the voice of our Good Shepherd. Jesus promised in John 10:27–29, "My sheep listen to my voice; I know them, and they follow me. I give them eternal life, and they shall never perish; no one can snatch them out of my hand. My Father, who has given them to me, is greater than all; no one can snatch them out of my Father's hand."

Jesus knows us! We may stumble at times. Occasionally, we may even miss His voice and lose a battle. But He promises us that the devil cannot snatch us out of God's eternal hand.

Understand Your Weapons

URING A WAR, AN ARMY that never attacks the enemy but only defends itself is fighting from a trapped position. It will never achieve victory on the defensive. Eventually the enemy will break through. Many Christians believe, and many preachers affirm, that the weapons listed in Ephesians 6:14–17 are intended only for defensive purposes, except for the sword of the Spirit. However, we are taught, "The weapons we fight with are not the weapons of the world. On the contrary, they have divine power to demolish strongholds" (2 Cor. 10:4). It is not possible to demolish a stronghold from a trapped, defensive position. Warriors must go on the offensive to triumph.

Jesus made it clear that human strength alone is not enough to prevail over demonic powers: "When a strong man, fully armed, guards his own house, his possessions are safe. But when someone stronger attacks and overpowers him, he takes away the armor in which the man trusted and divides up the spoils" (Luke 11:21–22). If we place our trust in worldly armor, such as material things, money, world systems, our socioeconomic position, or our power, rather than in God and His power and might and our spiritual armor, then the enemy can overpower us and take away the worldly armor in which we placed our trust. We have to learn how to protect our house and our family from being overtaken by the enemy. To do this, we must learn how to use the full array of spiritual armor and the weapons that God has given us to demolish the enemy's strongholds.

Spiritual Armor

The forge that shapes our spiritual armor is knowledge. God does all things after the counsel of His Word. Jesus said that if we remain in His Word, then we shall know the truth and be revealed as His disciples (John 15:7–8). This means we should:

- meditate on the Word of God

- memorize the Word of God

- obey the Word of God

- live the Word of God

- teach our children the Word of God

- proclaim the Word of God

As long as we are alive, problems are going to come our way. That is why we should do what God instructed: remain in His Word. Grasp it, believe it, obey it, and then watch it go into action. God watches over His Word to perform it (Jer. 1:12, NASB). No matter what obstacles we face, we should believe that God's Word is true. This belief is not "head knowledge;" it is "heart knowledge." We have to move from the mental realm of reason to the heart realm of faith.

It takes time and work to believe what God says in the face of life's challenges, but we should not give up. We have to learn to believe the promises of God's Word. Out of the abundance of our heart, our mouth will begin to speak faith. We can increase our faith by attending a church that teaches God's Word and supports us in our walk with the Lord. Have faith in God's almighty power and remember all things are possible for God. When we are rooted and grounded in God's Word, we can guard our house and ourselves and protect our most precious possessions, our family. Spiritual knowledge lays the foundation for understanding how to effectively use our spiritual weapons and armor.

Our Spiritual Weapons and Armor

In Ephesians 6:10–18, the apostle Paul writes about spiritual warfare in the life of believers and explains how to be victorious Christian soldiers.

> Finally, be strong in the Lord and in his mighty power. Put on the full armor of God so that you can take your stand against the devil's schemes. For our struggle is not against flesh and blood, but against the rulers, against the authorities, against the powers of this dark world and against the spiritual forces of evil in the heavenly realms. Therefore put on the full armor of God, so that when the day of evil comes, you may be able to stand your ground, and after you have done everything, to stand. Stand firm then, with the belt of truth buckled around your waist, with the breastplate of righteousness in place, and with your feet fitted with the readiness that comes from the gospel of peace. In addition to all this, take up the shield of faith, with which you can extinguish all the flaming arrows of the evil one. Take the helmet of salvation and the sword of the Spirit, which is the word of God. And pray in the Spirit on all occasions with all kinds of

> prayers and requests. With this in mind, be alert
> and always keep on praying for all the saints.

This Scripture brings closure to the apostle Paul's letter to the church at Ephesus. He begins with the word *finally* because in the previous passages he has outlined in detail how the spirit world affects Christians. He begins his letter by explaining the believer's redemption through the blood of Christ which, by grace, gives us the right to be seated together in heavenly places in Christ Jesus (Eph. 1:1–2:9). He then explains that Christ is seated at the right hand of God and has been given dominion over *every* principality, power, might, and dominion, and over every name that is named in all the ages to come (Eph. 1:20–23). He offers assurance that the Holy Spirit dwells within and empowers believers to accomplish God's purpose (Eph. 3:4–5, 16–19). He proclaims Christ's victory over death and hell and His supremacy over Satan (Eph. 4:8–10). He teaches them to walk in love, as Christ did (Eph. 5:2). Having reassured the church of its authority and position, the apostle Paul teaches them how to make war on the enemy.

Can you think of a time when you felt overwhelmed by life's challenges? Maybe you had a conflict with your spouse or your children, or maybe your retirement savings were dramatically reduced by an economic downturn or an unscrupulous financial advisor. Perhaps you lost your job and were faced with foreclosure on your home. These are the times when the enemy will try hardest to deceive you or discourage you. He will attempt to cast doubt on God's goodness. He will try to turn you away from prayer, from hope, and from faith in God. The enemy wants to catch you when you are off guard and most vulnerable. In times like these, it helps to understand spiritual warfare, so that you will be prepared for the enemy's attack before it happens.

God has provided Christian warriors with everything we

need to be victorious. There is no need to fear, because Jesus is Lord over all. Scripture tells us to be strong in the Lord and the power of His might. He will give us divine strength to resist the enemy. We need His power because we are not wrestling against flesh and blood but against powerful, cunning supernatural enemies. Jesus said, "Come to me, all you who are weary and burdened, and I will give you rest" (Matt. 11:28). Jesus offers rest to all who are troubled and weighted down with cares and worries; it is available if we only ask.

The apostle Paul used the word *wrestle* in Ephesians 6:12 (KJV) as a metaphor to portray the seriousness of our spiritual battle. At the time this epistle was written, Greek wrestlers fought vigorously because the loser of the wrestling match had his eyes gorged out, resulting in permanent blindness.[1] Although Paul was writing to the church, this metaphor applies to both Christians and non-Christians who fail to understand spiritual warfare. They are spiritually blinded. Their blindness causes them to be easy prey for the powers of darkness and spiritual forces of evil that can be manifested in flesh and blood by "the spirit who now works in the sons of disobedience" (Eph. 2:2, NKJV). Even though the attack is spiritual, it will be perpetrated by human beings. Those being attacked won't even see it coming.

According to Jesus, our battle is against "the prince of this world" (John 12:31; 14:30; 16:11). Satan exercises global influence, but he is not omnipresent, omnipotent, nor omniscient. He and his underlings are at work in every culture and society, and we need to prepare for their attacks. God has provided us with the armor necessary to withstand these attacks and extinguish every flaming arrow. Armed with the full armor of God and in the power of His might, we can take our stand against the works of the devil. Let's discuss how to do this in our daily lives.

STAND FIRM

After putting on our armor in preparation for the battle against the schemes, plans, and devices of the devil, we are told to stand, firm and fearless, against the enemy's assaults. The Scripture tells us, "When the day of evil comes, you may be able to stand your ground" (Eph. 6:13). The Scripture says "when," not "if." It's important to understand two things. One, the day of evil will come, bringing trials and tribulations. Second, we are standing on our own ground. We are in our own territory—our home, office, school, or church. Therefore our goal is to secure our area, stand firm, and not give any ground to the enemy.

In ancient times, the Spartans' famous strength derived from their ability to stand firm and use their shields to form a single impassable unit. Their shields were used defensively for protection and offensively for gaining ground. This is perfectly illustrated in a scene from the Warner Brothers movie *300*, which tells about three hundred Spartans who stood against the ancient Persian army. The Spartans' motto was "Give them nothing, but take from them everything."[2] At one point in the movie, the Persian army amasses a ground attack. The Spartans respond by using their shields as protection while moving forward and fighting the enemy in unison to break the enemy's line. By standing firm, they are able to move forward and prevail against the assault. Ultimately, the Spartans win that battle by forcing the Persians over a cliff into the sea below. When the Persians respond by firing thousands of arrows from a distance, the Spartans tighten their ranks, kneel together, and place their shields over themselves to form an impenetrable shelter.

The apostle Paul and the church at Ephesus would have been familiar with this method of fighting, because similar tactics were used by the Roman soldiers. Their elongated, round shields were designed to encourage tight ranks to form the Roman wedge, a tactic used while on the offensive. Two-thirds of each shield covered the body of its bearer from neck to thigh, and one-third covered the body of the soldier to his left from neck to thigh. The soldiers were dependent upon one another for protection. The same principle holds true for Christian soldiers. We need each other to succeed. Just like the Spartans and the Romans, when under attack Christians need to fight the battle in unison, kneel together in prayer, and protect themselves from harm with a spiritual covering. God has given us a shield to use both offensively and defensively as one of our spiritual weapons.

In our daily lives, giving in to temptation allows the enemy to enter our territory. Overcoming temptation requires self-discipline and a desire to obey God. God's Word assures us, "No temptation has seized you except what is common to man. And God is faithful; he will not let you be tempted beyond what you can bear. But when you are tempted, he will also provide a way out so that you can stand up under it" (1 Cor. 10:13).

There are many examples in the Bible of people being enticed by Satan to sin. Consider the following three cases. In each case, the person or persons tempted were given a way to withstand the temptation.

Adam and Eve, rather than listening to the serpent and disobeying God, could have gone to God and asked Him if what the serpent was saying were true (Gen. 3:1–13). One lesson we can learn from this example is that it is always wise to verify information and consider the source before taking action. Ask God to give you discernment to distinguish right from wrong and to recognize ungodly people for who they are.

King David, rather than listening to the wise counsel of a confidant and friend, also listened to Satan and ordered a census of Israel, even though he was warned not to do it (1 Chron. 21:1–4). The Scriptures tells us, "Satan rose up against Israel and incited

David to take a census of Israel" (v. 1). David was provided with a way to escape, but he did not listen. God places people in our lives to guide us and teach us to discern right and wrong. God gives us apostles, prophets, evangelists, pastors, teachers, and "the Spirit of wisdom and revelation" (Eph. 1:17), which helps us to know Him better. We have to learn to say no to temptation.

Ananias and Sapphira, rather than selling their property and letting Satan fill their hearts to lie about the price for which they sold it, could have kept their property (Acts 5:1–9). They allowed the desire to appear to be something they were not—generous, giving believers—to destroy them. Every lie comes from Satan.

There is a cost for defying God's authority. The devil will try to delude us into believing we can do anything we want without consequence. But true wisdom comes from knowing not only what we should do but also what we should not do.

Scripture tells us, "Anyone born of God does not continue to sin" (1 John 5:18). This does not mean that Christians won't be tempted or occasionally give in to temptation. It does mean that a Christian's life is changed by the indwelling of the Holy Spirit. Therefore, a Christian's lifestyle will not be gripped by uncontrollable sin. In every temptation, God provides a way out. Now let's examine the armor of God piece by piece so that we will understand how best to use it.

The Shield of Faith

The shield of faith is provided to block all the flaming arrows of the enemy (Eph. 6:16). In ancient times, flaming arrows were shot to kill, to burn, and to destroy those under attack. The fiery arrows of the enemy are metaphors for deception, doubt, condemnation, guilt, discouragement, debt, poverty, addictions, compulsions, and other insidious weapons in the devil's arsenal. They are intended to get God's people to trust something or someone other than God. Taking up our shield of faith means we believe and have confidence in God's power, His promises, and His assurance that we have been made righteous to Him through Jesus.

Our shield of faith forms an impenetrable barrier against the enemy's attacks when we are rooted and grounded in God's Word. We can increase our faith by surrounding ourselves with people and things that produce it. Our church should teach faith-building biblical principles, such as that it is God's will to heal us and not God's will for us to be poor or to suffer. Jesus told us He came so that we could have an abundant life, not only in heaven but right now (John 10:10, KJV). The Greek word for "abundant" is *perissos*. *Strong's Concordance* defines *perissos* as "superabundant in quantity, beyond measure, excessive, and superior in quality."[3] Churches that teach unbelief and try to place limits on God's almighty power do nothing but diminish faith and prevent believers from claiming their rightful inheritance as children of God, walking in the abundance Christ came for us to have.

God's Word says, "Without faith it is impossible to please God" (Heb. 11:6). To build our faith we cannot live in a negative atmosphere. We should surround ourselves with people who believe in the supernatural power of God. We should put ourselves in an environment that teaches faith, an environment in which miracles are taking place. God has not stopped performing miracles. We build our faith by sharing our testimonies of what God has done for us and for others. A wonderful example of a recent miracle is told in *A Miracle on the Road to Recovery*. This is a true story and a testament of faith concerning a man named John Keller, who was involved in an almost fatal motorcycle accident. This book is "the testimony of how his family's unquenchable love and unstoppable faith in the promises of God" brought John "through the miraculous healing of a traumatic brain injury."[4]

God is our Father. We must learn to walk in faith in the boldness we have as children of God. By trusting God's promises, His Word, and His timing without wavering, we can effectively use the shield of faith to overcome the daily challenges in our lives. Through our faith in Christ, we can go boldly and with confidence to the throne of grace and make our petitions known through prayer. God will hear us if we are living in obedience to His Word (Eph. 3:11–12; Phil. 4:6; 1 John 3:21–23). In every circumstance, even when we are hurting, we should find a Scripture that covers our particular situation and stand on that Scripture, boldly proclaiming what is ours and trusting in God's Word. Remember, we can do all things through Christ who strengthens us (Phil. 4:13, NKJV).

The Breastplate of Righteousness

The breastplate of righteousness is God's righteousness, which protects us. The breastplate of the Roman soldier was made of bronze. It covered the midsection of the body from the neck to the thighs. Its purpose was to protect the heart. Normally the soldier's shield warded off blows to the heart and other vital organs. But if the shield was lost or broken in the heat of battle, the breastplate served as a last line of defense to ward off a deadly blow to the heart. In modern times, it can be compared to equipment used by SWAT members or riot police approaching a hostile environment. They carry a metal shield and wear specially designed tactical vests that provide full protection for their torso. The tactical vest is a modern-day breastplate designed to protect the heart.

The apostle Paul used the metaphor of the breastplate to illustrate the necessity of protecting the most critical part of the body, the heart. The devil will often attack our heart in an attempt to cause us to be unfruitful. He wants to replace our love, joy, and peace with despair, guilt, and condemnation. The devil wants to rob Christians of the joy of God's salvation, and he often does it by causing us to feel we aren't good enough or righteous enough. He knows that if he can succeed it will impact our effectiveness as witnesses for the Lord. We read in Luke 6:45, "The good man brings good things out of the good stored up in his heart, and the evil man brings evil things out of the evil stored up in his heart. For out of the overflow of his heart his mouth speaks." What we believe in our heart dictates what we do and say.

Another way the devil tries to pierce our breastplate of righteousness is by attempting to convince us that we are not worthy of God's love and the love of others. He wants Christians to believe they are saved by works rather than by grace so that he can raise doubt about the quality and sincerity of their works. Roman Catholics and Mormons teach their parishioners that works are a fundamental component to earning one's place in heaven.

Many Christians go to church, tithe, or serve whenever called upon because they feel obligated. They live with condemnation and guilt because they are torn between what they want to do and what they think they have to do. The devil tugs at their hearts and continually inflicts emotional pain brought on by feelings of unworthiness. These unfortunate Christians believe they can't ever live well enough or do enough to merit God's favor. Satan's deception causes Christians to forget they are children of God who are righteous in His eyes through Christ.

Just as Noah became an "heir of the righteousness that comes by faith" (Heb. 11:7), Christians have become heirs by faith in Jesus. Our faith in Jesus makes us righteous before God, as Paul says: "God made him who had no sin to be sin for us, so that in him we might become the righteousness of God" (2 Cor. 5:21).

The righteousness of God transforms a Christian's life from god-lessness and wickedness to a life lived by faith (Rom. 1:17). We are assured, "If we confess our sins, [God] is faithful and just and will forgive us our sins and purify us from all unrighteousness" (1 John 1:9). This Scripture does not say we will be purified from only a part of our unrighteousness; it says "from all unrighteousness." As Pastor Ronnie Moore says, "All means all and that's all, all means."[5]

God is trustworthy. He will keep His covenant with us to purify us and cleanse us of all unrighteousness. If we confess our sins, the breastplate of righteousness will ward off the enemy's accusations that are intended to load us down with guilt, shame, and condemnation. The enemy cannot pierce our breastplate as long as we have it on. God has given us the protection we need for our heart. We have to do our part by believing God's Word and not doubting that we are righteous in God's eyes. We must believe we are saved by God's grace through faith in Jesus Christ and not by works. Salvation is a free gift from God (Eph. 2:8). It's true that we were created to do the good works which God prepared in advance for us to do (Eph. 2:10), but our works do not make us righteous before God.

All Christians are ministers of God, as the Bible says: "But in all things we commend ourselves as ministers of God: in much patience, in tribulations, in needs, in distresses....by purity, by knowledge, by longsuffering, by kindness, by the Holy Spirit, by sincere love, by the word of truth, by the power of God, by the *armor of righteousness* on the right hand and on the left" (2 Cor. 6:4, 6–7, NKJV, emphasis added). In the course of each day, nonbelievers observe us. We should take care to display at all times the attributes listed in the scripture above. The apostle Paul demonstrated these qualities during good times and bad, during success and tribulations, during freedom and imprisonment. Regardless of his circumstances or what others said about him, he remained a faithful minister of God. Not everyone agreed with Paul. Even some of the people in the church criticized him. We too should remain faithful ministers of God whether we receive praise or unfair criticism. We should not let our careless or undisciplined actions become another person's excuse for not accepting Jesus as Lord. Our lives are our witnesses. Be unoffendable.

The world will judge us by its own standards of righteousness. By living upright, loving, kind, honorable lives, in good times and in bad, we will give no place to the devil to attack our character. Be quick to listen, slow to speak, slow to become angry (James 1:19), and even slower to judge. For man's anger does not bring about the righteous life God desires (James 1:20).

The armor of righteousness on the right hand and on the left enables us to take a balanced approach to life's day-to-day challenges. And we are able to conduct ourselves in an exemplary manner in every aspect of our lives.

THE BELT OF TRUTH

The belt of truth buckled around your waist (Eph. 6:14) signifies that Christians need to be ready at all times to proclaim the truth, which is the gospel of our salvation (Eph. 1:13). Jesus is "the way and the truth and the life. No one comes to the Father except through [Him]" (John 14:6). Christians should listen to Jesus. He was born "to testify to the truth. Everyone on the side of truth listens to [Him]" (John 18:37). The belt of truth should be visible to others. Christians should live according to the gospel, meaning they should walk in the light, reflecting goodness, righteousness, and truth (Eph. 5:9). We should always speak the truth in love, with sincerity (Eph. 4:25).

Speaking the truth is a powerful defense against the devil's lies and deceit. One of the enemy's tactics is to try to get us to believe that truth is relative. It may begin with making compromises and telling white lies in the smallest of issues. However, when we don't keep our word, sooner or later our integrity becomes questionable. Proverbs 22:1 says, "A good name is more desirable than great riches," and Ecclesiastes 7:1 says, "A good name is better than fine perfume." Both Scriptures depict the value of integrity for men and women. This means that our interactions with others should be truthful and sincere. We should maintain the utmost integrity in all our dealings.

The belt of truth is also a metaphor for knowing the truth of God's Word. Knowledge of God's Word is a required offensive weapon that prevents Christians from being deceived by false leaders and teachers (Acts 20:28–31; 1 and 2 Tim.). False teaching can be demonic in origin (1 Tim. 4:1). The battle between truth and error is a major dimension of spiritual warfare, because false gospels are misleading and cause divisiveness and controversy. Satan's goal is to cause believers to "fall away from the faith" (1 Tim. 4:1, NAS). This is called apostasy, meaning renunciation of faith. Christians should read and study God's Word for themselves and not rely solely upon the instruction of others. The apostle Paul clearly warns believers to beware of "hypocritical liars" (1 Tim. 4:2) because they may abandon the faith and turn from God.

Our primary means of stopping the enemy in his tracks is to clothe ourselves in truth. We should be truthful with God, with ourselves, and with others. We should not compromise the truth, twist the truth, or rationalize our behavior under the guise of ignorance or relativism. There is no such thing as a white lie. Listen to the Holy Spirit. Be open to hearing and obeying Him. Be willing to admit when you are untruthful rather than hiding, denying, or shifting the blame to others. Own up to your faults without making excuses. Bring them before God and honestly confess them. The belt of truth is a sure-fire way to stand firm against deception. However, we can't just put it on and take it off when it suits us. We have to wear it at all times. The truth is a powerful weapon that will cause the enemy to flee.

THE SHOES FOR YOUR FEET

"Your feet fitted with the readiness that comes from the gospel of peace" means being ready to spread the good news of the gospel (Eph. 6:15). God wants Christians to be prepared to proclaim the gospel and the peace that is available through Jesus. *Readiness* means we should be firmly established in the assurance of our salvation in Jesus and be ready to share it with others. The devil will always attack grace and try to get people to doubt that Jesus paid the full price for our salvation. Many Christians hope that they will go to heaven if only they do their best while on Earth. Others believe they can do anything they want and live any way they want because atonement can be made for their sins after death.

The Church of Jesus Christ of Latter-Day Saints believes there is a spirit prison where people are sent after death based on the merits they earned in life. They also believe that a person's sins can be atoned for after death, even if the person knew and under-stood the Gospel and willingly rejected it. Under their teachings, a dead person who was in life a liar, a murderer, an adulterer, or worse can be redeemed from Hell. The person will suffer as a result of the full knowledge of their sins and choices, but atone-ment can be made for their sins after death at the end of the millennium. While they won't be admitted to the highest level of heaven, they will be free from hell. Their view of heaven is based on Section 76 of the Doctrine and Covenants and on their interpretation of 1 Corinthians 15.[6]

Roman Catholic doctrine teaches that good men, women, and

children who died without the knowledge of God can be sent to purgatory. Purgatory is "the state of those who die in God's friendship, assured of eternal salvation, but who still have need of purification to enter into the happiness of heaven."[7] This is according to the response to the question, "What is Purgatory?" published in 2005 in the *Compendium of the Catechism of the Catholic Church.*

These are just two examples of beliefs held by large organizations or, in the case of Catholicism, denominations of Christianity throughout the world that cause people to doubt that Jesus paid the full price for our salvation. Any doctrine that teaches that Jesus' life, death, and resurrection was insufficient to atone for all sins is in error. People who believe their works can get them into heaven, or even worse, that their lawlessness can be atoned for after their deaths, are being deceived by Satan. Jesus tells us everyone practicing evil hates the light and is condemned (John 3:19–20). God "did not spare his own Son, but gave him up for us all" (Rom. 8:32). Considering the high cost of our salvation—the blood of God's own son—why should anyone believe they could reject the gospel, practice evil, and still go to heaven?

The apostle Paul teaches in the Book of Galatians that we are not to use the freedom we receive in Christ to live sinful lives (Gal. 5:13). He warns that those who do will not inherit the kingdom of God (vv. 19–21). If we try to justify ourselves, we will be alienated from Christ and fall away from grace (v. 4). In Ephesians 2:8–9 we read, "For it is by grace you have been saved, through faith—and this not from yourselves, it is the gift of God—not by works, so that no one can boast." Clearly, works without grace will not save us. There is no merit system by which we can save ourselves. We must have faith in Christ and believe that only by grace are we saved.

The Bible is very clear that Jesus is the Son of God and that

He is the only way to get into heaven. "For God so loved the world that He gave His only begotten Son, that whoever believes in Him should not perish but have everlasting life. For God did not send His Son into the world to condemn the world, but that the world through Him might be saved" (John 3:16–17, NKJV).

This is God's testimony about His Son: "God has given us eternal life, and this life is in His Son. He who has the Son has life; he who does not have the Son of God does not have life" (1 John 5:11–12, NKJV). Jesus says, "I am the way and the truth and the life. No one comes to the Father except through me" (John 14:6).

Christians must know, without a doubt, the good news of Jesus Christ inside and out. This is one of our most powerful weapons, because evangelism is the Great Commission from Jesus Christ. He told us to go and make disciples of all nations (Matt. 28:19). The devil will do everything he can to cast doubt on the gospel to keep people from Christ, but we have God's assurance that as believers in His Son, we have eternal life. We should always be ready to boldly proclaim the gospel of peace.

Jesus tells us that in Him we "may have peace" despite living in a world that will bring us trouble because He has "overcome the world" (John 16:33). This promise of peace is very comforting. We are at war. However, we can take heart knowing that Jesus is our peace and that He has already defeated the devil (Eph. 2:14).

THE HELMET OF SALVATION

The helmet of salvation protects a believer's mind from doubting God's promises. "The god of this age has blinded the minds of unbelievers, so that they cannot see the light of the gospel of the glory of Christ, who is the image of God" (2 Cor. 4:4). The helmet of salvation protects Christians from doubts about

God's acceptance of them, in spite of the sins they have committed while their minds were blinded to the truth. It also guards a believer's mind from doubting thoughts about whether he or she is truly saved.

We have assurance of our salvation through Jesus. Romans 10:9 tells us, "If you confess with your mouth, 'Jesus is Lord,' and believe in your heart that God raised him from the dead, you will be saved." The gospel is the truth. It is a fact. But the devil will try to plant doubts in our minds by asking, "Do you really believe in your heart?" Or he might say, "How can you really be sure you believe enough?" Or he may ask, "What if you're wrong?"

This battle is for the mind. The devil wants us to question or doubt God. If a thought causes anxiety, fear, or doubt, you can be certain that it is not from the Holy Spirit but from an evil spirit. The Holy Spirit never causes us to doubt God. The enemy will also plant hateful or lustful thoughts in our minds—thoughts that seem to come out of nowhere—or tempt us to use profanity, although we don't usually curse. When this happens, we can rebuff his attacks by meditating on God's Word; listening to gospel music; praising and worshiping God; memorizing Scripture; or simply by reciting Scripture in the first tense, such as, "I demolish arguments and every pretension that sets itself up against the knowledge of God, and I take captive every thought to make it obedient to Christ" (2 Cor. 10:5).

Declaring God's Word is very effective against the enemy, and 2 Corinthians 10:5 is an excellent scripture to memorize to readily take control of your thoughts. God has given us a helmet of salvation to protect our minds, but we can't do it alone. We need God's help—which is why it is important to memorize Scripture verses. Filling our minds with Scripture gives us the ability to take authority over any situation in our lives by using

God's Word and to stop all spiritual forces of evil within our sphere of influence.

We will discuss the power of declaring and decreeing God's Word in our discussion of our next weapon, the sword of the Spirit.

THE SWORD OF THE SPIRIT

"The sword of the Spirit, which is the Word of God" means that the Holy Spirit is the power behind the Christian warrior's use of the Word of God (Eph. 6:17). The Holy Spirit is the awesome power of God. The Holy Spirit is the Teacher and Spirit of truth sent from the Father (John 14:26). In the Book of Isaiah we read that the Holy Spirit is the Spirit of wisdom, understanding, counsel, power, and knowledge (Isa. 11:2). He will make the Word come alive in your spirit.

God's Word, when it is alive in you, will transform your mind and lifestyle. Others will notice the change and seek your advice. Then you can minister to them, offering spiritual guidance and support. Faith always has a good report, so speak words that strengthen, encourage, and comfort. Another role for warriors is to bear up one another during difficult times. The Holy Spirit will provide wise counsel on what to say to your brothers and sisters in Christ and how to say it.

The apostle Paul informs us that the Holy Spirit is the Spirit of holiness, through whom Jesus "was declared with power to be the Son of God" (Rom. 1:4). The apostle John tells us the Holy Spirit is the voice of God to the churches (Rev. 2:7). Christians are to trust in the truth of God's Word. Jesus referred to the Holy Spirit as the Spirit of truth who will guide us into all truth spoken by God (John 16:13).

Jesus spoke God's Word when He was confronted by the devil (Matt. 4:1–11), and we should do likewise. When He defeated

Satan, He responded to each of Satan's temptations by saying, "It is written." When Satan attempts to test you, remember that he is defeated by the blood of the Lamb and the word of our testimony (Rev. 12:11). Through the power of the Holy Spirit we are able to memorize Scripture and speak God's Word to resist and rebuke the devil. The Holy Spirit was sent by God to teach us all things and to help us remember what we have been taught (John 14:26). He abides in us to comfort, strengthen, and encourage us. He will remind us of God's Word to help us when we are discouraged or distressed, thereby building our faith.

In Revelation, Jesus wages war with the sword of His mouth (Rev. 1:16; 2:12, 16; 19:15). We too should wage war with the sword of His Word. In *Ministry of the Holy Spirit in the Last Days,* Pastor Ronnie Moore writes, "Guidance for the believer should begin with the written Word of God. The Bible records the will of God for His people. As a believer obeys the Word, he is moving in the direction of God's plan for his life. Therefore, if one knows God's Word concerning a certain subject, then he will immediately know God's will."[8] God accomplishes His will through His Word. His Word will not return to Him void (Isa. 55:11). God's Word has the power to do what He says it will do. When we wage war with the sword of the Spirit, which is the Word of God, we cannot fail.

FULL ARMOR OF GOD

As you can see, God has given us everything we need to stand firm against demonic attacks. But if we ignore Scripture's warning to put on the full armor of God, we give the devil an undeserved advantage. When his attack comes, we will not be prepared to protect ourselves. The full armor of God is not intended for use only when trouble arises. It should be worn daily and become a lifestyle. Each element provides divine safeguards for every circumstance that may arise in our lives. Difficult times may come, but we can consciously and vigorously stand our ground. Becoming aware of and preparing prior to the attacks can help us succeed in our battles.

AUTHORITY: OUR ULTIMATE WEAPON

We can confront every demonic attack by exercising the authority we have as Christians. We can say, "By the authority of Jesus Christ and under the protection of His shed blood, I command you, demon, be gone!" Satan is powerless against the authority and blood of Jesus. In the name of Jesus, Christians have the authority to command spiritual opponents to leave their sphere of influence—and they *must* go (James 4:7). But our enemy will not go away permanently. He will lick his wounds and look for another way to advance. Even so, we have the assurance that we can face our daily battles and live victorious lives by exercising our authority.

An excellent book on the authority we have over evil spirits through Jesus Christ is *The Believer's Authority* by Kenneth E. Hagin. In this book, Reverend Hagin responds to the question, "Do we have authority that we don't know about—that we haven't discovered—that we're not using?" Yes, we do. Reverend Hagin tells us we must depend on the Holy Spirit to help in ministering this authority. He tells us we are helpless without both the Spirit and the Word of God; we cannot exercise this authority by ourselves.[9]

Reverend Hagin states, "Our combat with the devil always should be with the consciousness that we have authority over him because he is a defeated foe—the Lord Jesus Christ defeated him for us....We receive this authority when we are born again." He also writes, "Although we have authority over demon spirits, we do not have authority over our fellow men or their wills....We have authority over demons, and we can control them as far as our lives or our family's lives are concerned, but we can't always control them when other people are concerned, because that person's will comes into play."[10]

Some people willingly choose to invite demons into their lives by participating in occult activities. Others may choose to live with them for other reasons, as in the case below. Even though a Christian may have a desire to deliver such a person from demonic oppression, they won't be able to because the person has given the demon permission to be in his or her life. I witnessed an example of this on a mission trip to Aguascalientes, Mexico. There was a woman attending the church revival service in whom an evil spirit manifested. Attempts to deliver this woman from the evil spirit were unsuccessful because she refused to renounce Satan. She did not want to let it go. We found out later that she was a prostitute who was married and had children. We were told that she was tormented by her lifestyle and did not believe it was possible for God to love her. Satan is such a liar! Another woman in the same service was set free from an evil spirit when she renounced Satan and accepted Jesus as Lord over her life. The instantaneous, miraculous transformation in her countenance and demeanor were astounding. I will never forget her exuberance as she joyfully jumped around, dancing and praising God.

Demons are real. But we have spiritual weapons to meet the enemy head-on and take our stand against them in the power and might of God. And we have the delegated authority from Jesus to cast out demons in His name. We are assured of success because Jesus declared of His disciples, "In my name they will drive out demons" (Mark 16:17). When a spirit of doubt says, "You can't do that;" or a spirit of pride says, "You can handle that by yourself, you don't need God;" or a spirit of unforgiveness says, "That person betrayed you, you can never forgive her for that," stand against that evil spirit and rebuke it in the name of Jesus. Then don't give it another thought.

Each time you hear an internal voice that causes fear, anxiety, depression, anger, resentment, bitterness, guilt, or condemnation, know that it is an evil spirit and rebuke it immediately. Don't entertain the thought! Do you want to entertain evil spirits? Of course you don't, so don't entertain ungodly thoughts. Take those thoughts captive and make them obedient to Christ.

God has equipped us with everything we need to prevail (John 3; Eph. 6:10–18; 1 Cor. 12–14). We have Jesus on our side, who is Lord over all (Eph. 1:21–23). We can confidently stand our ground fully armed and set for battle. There is power in the name of Jesus!

Overcoming the Enemy

You may have to fight a
battle more than once to win it.
Margaret Thatcher[1]

S OME BATTLES MUST BE FOUGHT more than once, each time with the intent of winning, before the victory is won. The devil's fate is sealed, and he knows his final outcome; however, he has not decided just to lie down and accept defeat. He has declared war on mankind. He is doing everything he can to thwart God's plan for redemption. He aggressively pursues all non-Christians to keep them from becoming believers. And he does everything he can to confuse and nullify the efforts of Christians to live godly lives. Spiritual battles are a part of everyday life. Although you may have fought your current battle before, you should not give up. This may be the last time you will need to fight this battle to win it.

Just as in any war, in the struggle between the kingdom of heaven and the powers of darkness each individual is either on one side or the other. You're either for God or against Him. There is no neutral zone, no in-between. Jesus said, "Everyone who does evil hates the light, and will not come into the light for fear that his deeds will be exposed" (John 3:20). He also said, "He who is not with me is against me" (Matt. 12:30). The battle lines have been drawn. We each must decide whether to push the enemy back or invite the enemy in.

Satan does not want you to know that he is vying for control of your life. He wants you to continue to live in denial. He does not want you to choose sides because he is afraid you will choose Jesus. He wants you to believe there is no heaven or hell. Armed with this belief, you can live your life any way you choose, trusting that there will be no consequences after death. But Satan is a liar. Heaven is real. Hell is real. Everyone must choose. You cannot stay on the sidelines. Everyone will spend eternity somewhere. The question is, Where will you spend it?

Give the Enemy No Opportunity

When I was growing up, one of my favorite cartoons was *The Road Runner Show*. Week after week, Wile E. Coyote tried to capture the Road Runner. Though he was constantly thwarted in his efforts, he relentlessly came back with new devices to achieve his goal. Satan is the same way. He will never stop trying to find an open door in our lives through which to enter, his sole purpose being "to steal and kill and destroy" (John 10:10).

Unlike the Road Runner, we may not always see our enemy's traps in advance and find a way to avoid them. His methods are subtle. We may not recognize tactics, such as pride, greed, lust, and drug or alcohol addictions, which give him a foothold in our lives.

Worldly wisdom would tell us that we are in control and that supernatural forces of evil are not influencing us to succumb to these tactics. But is it possible that we don't have the spiritual discernment to recognize the origin of these attacks?

To achieve victory over the enemy, we must learn how to discern God's will and wisdom for whatever circumstance we are going through and then implement a plan of action to take control of the situation using godly wisdom. We must ask ourselves, Is it possible that an evil spirit is behind this circumstance? And if so, what evil spirit is it? Battles are easier to fight when we understand what we're up against. If we don't know what we are fighting, we will invariably be defeated in battle.

Jesus knew God's will and came to Earth to fulfill God's plan. He understood who the enemy was and how to defeat him and his armies. Jesus won the war against Satan when He was crucified and resurrected from the dead. Satan's final outcome is explained in the Book of Revelation. Jesus will cast "the devil, who deceived them...into the lake of fire and brimstone" where he "will be tormented day and night forever and ever" (Rev. 20:10, NKJV). It's important to note that the verse says, "The devil, who deceived them." Scripture clearly tells us that people will be deceived by Satan. Knowing this, everyone needs to be on alert and prepared for Satan's deception and lies.

There is one battle that Satan cannot win. He cannot destroy a Christian's relationship with Jesus. The apostle Paul writes, "Who shall separate us from the love of Christ? Shall trouble or hardship or persecution or famine or nakedness or danger or sword?...No, in all these things we are more than conquerors through him who loved us. For I am convinced that neither death nor life, neither angels nor demons, neither the present nor the future, nor any powers, neither height nor depth, nor anything else in all creation, will be able to separate us from the love of God that is in Christ Jesus our Lord" (Rom. 8:35, 37–39).

Salvation entered the world through Jesus, God's Son. Because of the devil's desire to destroy everything good and keep people from accepting the free gift of salvation, we are in a spiritual battle. Sin and salvation are the reasons that spiritual warfare is taking place on Earth.

Knowing that he cannot destroy our relationship with Christ

Jesus, the devil tries to oppress us and keep us from fulfilling God's plans for our lives. He tempts us in an effort to get us out of God's favor. However, we must say no to temptation and ask for God's help when we are tempted.

CONFRONTING TEMPTATION

The Amplified Bible gives the following interpretation of James 1:13–15: "Let no one say when he is tempted, I am tempted from God; for God is incapable of being tempted by [what is] evil and He Himself tempts no one. But every person is tempted when he is drawn away, enticed and baited by his own evil desire (lust, passions). Then the evil desire, when it has conceived, gives birth to sin, and sin, when it is fully matured, brings forth death."

This scripture depicts the process of temptation. First, Satan or one of his demons plants an idea in our minds. Second, we allow ourselves to dwell on that idea and fantasize or daydream about it. Third, we justify it and form rationalizations as to why we should go through with it. And finally, we give in.

We have the power and authority to capture every thought and yield it to Christ. Scripture tells us to "demolish arguments and every pretension that sets itself up against the knowledge of God" and to "take captive every thought to make it obedient to Christ" (2 Cor. 10:5). When we are exposed to ideas that might lead to sinful desires, we can choose either to recognize the danger and refocus our thoughts or to let ourselves be ensnared by our fantasies. We can rely on the Holy Spirit to guide us and direct us. We can obey the Word of God in Proverbs: "Trust in the LORD with all your heart and lean not on your own understanding; in all your ways acknowledge him, and he will make your paths straight" (Prov. 3:5–6).

God's Word tells us that if we resist the devil and stand firm in faith, then the devil will flee. Satan does everything he can to lead us into temptation and away from God. He wants to stop people from knowing the truth about God's one and only Son, Jesus. Because he is so skillful at deception, there are more non-Christians in the world than Christians. Even in the United States, a Christian nation, Satan is gaining ground. He is doing everything he can to supplant good with evil. Ungodly philosophies and rebellious attitudes are currently threatening to overtake our society.

Knowledge and Good Judgment

Every year, new laws are enacted to legalize and to sanction ungodly philosophies and unethical principles. The proponents of these new laws are willing to make their arguments before the U.S. Supreme Court, if necessary, in an attempt to overthrow godly wisdom in favor of worldly wisdom.

One example of this is the growing interest in human cloning. Human cloning is the laboratory production of individuals who are genetically identical to existing human beings. Cloning is achieved by putting the genetic material from a donor into a woman's egg that has had its nucleus removed. As a result, the new or cloned embryo is an identical copy of the donor, having no genetic contribution from the woman who gives birth to the child.

In 1997, in response to the successful cloning of Dolly the sheep, President Clinton asked the National Bioethics Advisory Commission (NBAC) to review the profound ethical issues raised by the possible cloning of human beings. The commission found unanimously that it was morally unacceptable for anyone to attempt to create a child with the technology used to create Dolly the sheep. Acting on the commission's key recommendation, President Clinton signed the Cloning Prohibition Act of 1997, banning the use of somatic cell nuclear transfer technology for the purpose of cloning human beings. President Clinton's ban called for a five-year moratorium on human cloning. He directed the NBAC to report to the president in four and one-half years on whether the ban should continue.[2]

During the five-year moratorium, President George W. Bush was elected. Prior to the expiration of the moratorium, President Bush upheld the continuation of the ban. In a speech given at the White House, he said:

> Allowing cloning would be taking a significant step toward a society in which human beings are grown for spare body parts, and children are engineered to custom specifications; and that's not acceptable.
>
> I believe all human cloning is wrong, and ought to be banned, for the following reasons.
>
> First, anything other than a total ban on human cloning would be unethical....
>
> Secondly, anything other than a total ban on human cloning would be virtually impossible to enforce. Cloned human embryos created for research would be widely available in laboratories and embryo farms....Even the tightest regulations and strict policing would not prevent or detect the birth of cloned babies.
>
> Third, the benefits of research cloning are highly speculative. Yet even if research cloning were medically effective, every person who wanted to benefit would need an embryonic clone of his or her own, to provide the designer tissues. This would create a massive national market for eggs and egg donors, and exploita-

tion of women's bodies that we cannot and must
not allow.[3]

The 1997 NBAC report concluded, however, that the cloning
of DNA, cells, tissues, and non-human animals using somatic
cell nuclear transfer and other cloning techniques was not ethi-
cally problematic when conducted in compliance with existing
regulations and guidelines, thus leaving the door open for Satan
to devise a plan to scientifically create humans.[4]

In January 2009, President Bush's term expired and Barack
Obama took office as president. On March 9, 2009, President
Obama signed an executive order reversing the Bush-era stem
cell policy. But the president was insistent that his order would
not open the door to human cloning. During his speech at the
White House announcing the change in policy, he stated:

> We will develop strict guidelines, which we
> will rigorously enforce, because we cannot ever
> tolerate misuse or abuse....And we will ensure
> that our government never opens the door to
> the use of cloning for human reproduction. It is
> dangerous, profoundly wrong, and has no place
> in our society, or any society.[5]

President Obama also signed a presidential memorandum
directing the head of the White House Office of Science and
Technology Policy to: (1) develop a strategy for restoring scientific integrity to governmental decision-making and (2) appoint
scientific advisors based on their credentials and experience, not
their politics or ideology.[6]

The second element of this mandate may be difficult to accomplish, because while a person's politics are often known, their
thoughts and beliefs may not be as apparent. Protecting free and

open inquiry without giving any regard to a person's ideology does not ensure that the data will not be skewed. Data is only as good as those that collect it. President Obama made a promise that "no data will be distorted or concealed to protect a political agenda."[7] No such promise was made regarding ideology.

This issue will most certainly go before Congress, because President Obama asked them to "act on a bi-partisan basis to provide further support for this research."[8] During their debates, our Congressmen will be called upon to decide if our moral development has kept pace with our technological development. They will be challenged to determine whether we are capable of protecting ourselves from the irresponsible use of technology. They will be responsible for deciding whether scientists can be trusted to properly use this technology or whether President Bush's concern that "even the tightest regulations and strict policing would not prevent or detect the birth of cloned babies" was a prophetic declaration.

Considering that the benefits of research into cloning are highly speculative and the drawbacks are potentially diabolic, the outcome of this battle could be catastrophic. Although God created man and woman to have dominion over and populate the Earth, Satan is doing everything he can to counterfeit God's plan for creation. The Bible warns us to give no place to Satan. In the power of our might we can do nothing, but in the power of the Holy Spirit we can learn how to disarm Satan and break the grip of his growing stronghold over our nation.

SPIRITUAL STRONGHOLDS

Spiritual strongholds can result from being in agreement with a lie. They can prevent us from walking into the destiny that God has for us. When we allow ourselves to be controlled by incorrect perceptions, we risk succumbing to the negative side of Proverbs

23:7: "For as he thinks within himself, so he is" (NAS). For example, if we believe we are stupid or selfish or reprehensible or unredeemable, we are allowing the enemy to gain ground and establish a spiritual stronghold in our mind.

Not only do our thoughts ensnare us, but so do words. We advance the kingdom of darkness with critical, cruel, untruthful words, such as gossip. In Proverbs 6:2 we are warned, "You are snared by the words of your mouth" (NKJV). Many of us are in bondage because of words we have spoken or because of the words of others. We often speak word-curses over ourselves and over others by saying destructive things like, "You're stupid," "You're so lazy," or, "I'm so worthless; I'll never amount to anything." We can advance God's kingdom with words of encouragement, edification, and praise. We need to learn how to speak as God desires to avoid harming ourselves or others.

Fortunately, it is clear from the following scripture that we have a supernatural arsenal with which we can demolish spiritual strongholds: "The weapons we fight with are not the weapons of the world. On the contrary, they have divine power to demolish strongholds. We demolish arguments and every pretension that sets itself up against the knowledge of God, and we take captive every thought to make it obedient to Christ" (2 Cor. 10:4–5). This weaponry includes prayer, faith, hope, love, self-control, God's Word, and the Holy Spirit. This artillery can smash not only proud, worldly arguments that defy God but also false perceptions about who we are.

Ed Silvoso, president of Harvest Evangelism, defines a spiritual stronghold as "a mind-set impregnated with hopelessness that leads us to accept as unchangeable situations that we know are contrary to the will of God." According to him, spiritual strongholds are built in the mind "by Satan so he can manipulate behavior without being detected."[9]

Delusion, duplicity, betrayal, beguilement, and deception—the weapons of the devil—all involve deliberate concealment, distortions, or misrepresentations. These can cause a person to believe something that is not true and can lead that person into error, danger, despair, or a disadvantageous position. Manipulative behavior can be accomplished by pleasant, alluring methods, or bold-faced lies. Unknowingly, we can let false perceptions control our beliefs about ourselves and the world around us. Although they are false, they still have power.

It is frequently said, "Our perceptions are our reality." We are who we are because of what we allow ourselves to think, which is why it is important to guard our minds. It is equally important to be careful with whom we associate because "'bad company corrupts good character'" (1 Cor. 15:33). If we surround ourselves with permissive people, we will become permissive. If we surround ourselves with negative people, we will become negative. Relationships are important, as evidenced by the life of King Solomon. The wisest and richest king ever to live (2 Chron. 9:22–23), Solomon knew God personally, yet he married idol worshipers and became one himself (1 Kings 11:1–11). In Ecclesiastes, Solomon wrote about how he had been deceived into pursuing meaningless pleasures, all for nothing. In the end, he concluded, "Fear God and keep his commandments, for this is the whole duty of man. For God will bring every deed into judgment, including every hidden thing, whether it is good or evil" (Eccles. 12:13–14).

OVERCOMING SPIRITUAL STRONGHOLDS

One way a person can overcome spiritual strongholds is to stand on the promises of God and decree and declare them when a spirit of doubt or rejection manifests itself. The promises of God to us, which are found in His Word, let us know who we are and why we can be victorious in the battle against the enemy.

When we personalize scriptures by confessing them in the first person, God's Word comes alive in us. *Prayers That Avail Much* by Germaine Copeland is filled with prayers that do this. One of the prayers is for overcoming a feeling of rejection, and it contains some of God's promises about who we are as heirs of His kingdom. The following prayer can help you overcome spiritual strongholds.

> *Heavenly Father, I worship and adore You. In spite of the rejection I have experienced, I declare that Your eyes are upon me, and I am righteous before You through Christ Jesus. Your ears are attentive to my prayers, and everything You say about me in Your Word is true:*
>
> *I am blessed with all spiritual blessing in heavenly places in Christ (Eph. 1:3).*
>
> *I am chosen by You, my Father; and am holy and without blame (Eph. 1:4).*
>
> *I am Your child according to the good pleasure of Your will (Eph. 1:5).*
>
> *I am redeemed through the blood of Jesus (Eph. 1:7).*
>
> *I am an heir (Eph. 1:11).*
>
> *I have a spirit of wisdom and revelation in the knowledge of Christ (Eph. 1:17).*
>
> *I am saved by Your grace (Eph. 2:5).*
>
> *I am of Your household; I am a citizen of heaven (Eph. 2:19).*
>
> *I am strengthened with might by Your Spirit (Eph. 3:16).*
>
> *I am rooted and grounded in love (Eph. 3:17)*
>
> *I am more than a conqueror (Rom. 8:37).*
>
> *I am an overcomer (Rev. 12:11).*

I am free (John 8:36).
I am victorious (1 John 5:4).

Everything You say about me is true, Lord. In Your Name, Jesus, I pray. Amen.[10]

Praying scriptures builds our faith and develops a more intimate relationship with God. These promises let us know who we are and why we can be victorious in the battle against the enemy. They also help to explain why Satan hates us so much and will always be our enemy. He knows we have a future as citizens of heaven, through Christ Jesus, that he will never have. Knowing this, we can confidently develop strategies to effectively take our stand and live victoriously.

Jesus is Lord over my spirit, my soul, and my body (Phil. 2:9–11)!

Prepare Your Children for Spiritual Warfare

*T*HE FAMILY, AND ESPECIALLY CHILDREN, are under attack in these times. Daily we can read news reports about the increase in teenage pregnancies, high school dropouts, and drug problems among American youth. The family seems to have become Satan's number one target. Satan attacks our families in many ways, some of which I have just mentioned, and all of which are intended to achieve the breakdown of the family structure. Many households are now run by single parents. The divorce rate has risen from generation to generation, and family structures have changed. The home is the primary environment in which to teach and learn spiritual lessons and the way to live godly lives. Our families are under attack because Satan knows the family is important to God. Our goal is to protect our families and help our children become strong, active Christians and good citizens and role models for society.

LEARNING BY DOING

During a vacation with my family in September 2007, we stopped at a roadside restaurant for lunch. Two women and a man were seated at the booth behind us. I happened to overhear portions of their conversation. From what I could gather, these individuals were concerned because some members of their church wanted the training they received "to be more practical than spiritual."

They expressed concern that many of the members with children "want to go for more practical than spiritual guidance." I heard one of them say, "We need people who don't have children to teach the children." The man suggested, "We need to get older people to teach the children more spiritual aspects."

What I was able to construe from the conversation was that in order to keep the youth interested and involved, teachings at the church had become more practical, and lessons were being taught from a practical rather than a spiritual point of view. The individuals seated behind me seemed to be concerned that the youth were not being taught how to apply the Bible to their daily lives. The lessons had strayed from a firm foundation in the principles taught in Scripture and were no longer about putting these principles into practice. These individuals seemed to be wrestling with spiritual opponents in the church who wanted to water down the gospel. It sounded as if they were in need of guidance to develop strategies to equip themselves and their children to win the spiritual battle they were fighting.

Sometimes it can be difficult to connect Scriptures to our day-to-day lives, and therefore many teachers shy away from teaching all but what is easily understood. Sometimes the teacher may be afraid of the questions, So what? What does that have to do with today? Satan loves to challenge us when we teach God's Word, which is why it is important to know and understand its timeless truths. One way to approach God's Word is to make it personal by asking, "What does it mean to me, my family, my children, my church, or my friends?" This can show us how to apply it to the problems and pressures that arise in our lives and enable us to make it meaningful and relevant for ourselves without compromising its truth.

The inability or unwillingness of some churches to properly instruct our youth only increases the importance of teaching and applying spiritual principles in the home. If our children see us doing the right thing, they will learn by the example we set. We must demonstrate on a daily basis how to handle tests, trials, and tribulations in a godly way. Succumbing to lukewarm, politically correct teaching impairs our children by leading them to believe they can pick and choose which portions of the Bible to follow. Believing this, they may begin to model their lives after the world as it fits their needs or desires. Eventually, it may cause them to question the infallibility of the Bible.

Some churches avoid speaking about homosexuality, adultery, witchcraft, the occult, or other controversial topics found in the Bible because they are afraid they will lose members. But have they considered the effect their decisions will have on our children? Church leaders who turn a blind eye to specific sections of the Bible because someone may be offended by them or because speaking about them could shrink the numbers of their congregations are putting our next generation at risk of growing up to believe that it is better to be politically correct than to obey God. Teaching from a spiritual point of view enables our children to make wise decisions that will have lifelong favorable outcomes.

As we raise up the next generation, we must not bury our heads in the sand because of our own fears. We need to train our children so that they will recognize good from evil and not be unaware of Satan's devices. The Lord wants us to prepare our children to receive divine revelation to guide their lives.

HONOR YOUR FATHER AND MOTHER

As children mature into adolescence, they are continually bombarded with direct assaults from the enemy in the form of peer pressure and immoral influences from a variety of sources—radio, television, the Internet, and video games chief among them—that can cause them to rebel against their parents and the church. It is important to teach biblical truths and godly wisdom to children at an early age so that they will be armored against these harmful influences as they grow into maturity. We should always remember that our children watch how we handle situations; therefore, we ought to model what we teach.

Beginning as toddlers and throughout their childhood, children should be taught God's promise for being obedient to one's parents. In Ephesians 6:1–3, we read, "Children, obey your parents in the Lord, for this is right. 'Honor your father and mother'—which is the first commandment with a promise—'that it may go well with you and that you may enjoy long life on the earth.'" If we raise our children to know what is right and to be obedient, and they are faithful to do it, then, God promises, it will go well with them. They will enjoy long life on Earth.

To clearly understand this promise, I looked up the Greek word for "may" from the King James Version of this verse in *Strong's Concordance*. The word translated "may" comes from the Greek word *esomai,* which means, "shall be; will be; shall come to pass."[1] God's promise to children for honoring their father and mother is that it *shall* go well with them and they *shall* enjoy long life on Earth. *It shall come to pass!* This is a promise every parent should want for their children.

AGE OF UNDISCIPLINED PERMISSIVENESS

In many homes, both parents work full-time jobs and are not at home when their children return from school. And when the parents do arrive, they are often kept busy preparing dinner or performing other activities, which leaves their children managing their own time with minimal oversight. Without establishing parental controls, many parents have no idea what their children are watching or listening to in the various forms of uncensored media available to them. Children are naturally curious, and Satan uses this curiosity to tempt them. Unless you closely monitor children's television programs, music, DVDs, and Internet access, they are able to slip into a state of undisciplined permissiveness.

This state of permissiveness can be very dangerous. In *A Parent's Guide to Internet Safety,* an online pamphlet published by the Federal Bureau of Investigation to help parents understand the complexities of online child exploitation, Louis J. Freeh, the former director of the FBI writes:

> Our children are our Nation's most valuable asset. They represent the bright future of our country and hold our hopes for a better Nation. Our children are also the most vulnerable members of society....Unfortunately the same advances in computer and telecommunication technology that allow our children to reach out to new sources of knowledge and cultural experiences are also leaving them vulnerable to exploitation and harm by computer-sex offenders.[2]

This pamphlet describes how predators can manipulate and seduce children online through the use of attention, affection, kindness, and even gifts. During online chats, these individuals will spend time listening to and empathizing with the child's problems, concerns, hopes, and dreams in an attempt to establish a relationship and build trust. These individuals will be aware of the latest music, movies, teen idols, hobbies, and interests of children in order to communicate on their level. They attempt to gradually lower children's inhibitions by slowly introducing sexual context and content into their conversations. This pamphlet warns:

It is important for parents to understand that children can be indirectly victimized through conversation, i.e. "chat," as well as the transfer of sexually explicit information and material. Parents and children should remember that a computer-sex offender can be any age or sex.

Children, especially adolescents, are sometimes interested in and curious about sexuality and sexually explicit material. They may be moving away from the total control of parents and seeking to establish new relationships outside their family. Because they may be curious, children/adolescents sometimes use their on-line access to actively seek out such materials and individuals.

Some adolescent children may also be attracted to and lured by on-line offenders closer to their age who, although not technically child molesters, may be dangerous.[3]

Internet predators often pretend to be children or teenagers in order to lure children into unsafe environments. The above pamphlet was prepared from actual investigations involving child victims and from actual cases where law enforcement officers posed as children. Anyone who has any knowledge about these criminals should contact their local FBI office in the United States or local law enforcement, if living outside the United States.

As stated above by former FBI Director Freeh, children are the most valuable and vulnerable members of our society. Satan knows this, and he devises evil plans to harm children. He influences people from all walks of life to prey upon children. To protect children from Internet predators, computers should be placed in areas of the house that can be seen by other family members, instead of in the child or teenager's bedroom. Children may pout or throw a temper tantrum to resist having the computer in a conspicuous location. However, by forcing children to use the computer in full view of others, parents can minimize the effects of undisciplined permissiveness and establish a hedge of protection against Satan's attacks.

If, as a parent, you have decided to succumb to your child's desires to have a computer in his bedroom because you trust him, then be sure to establish parental controls with your service provider to prevent predators from having access to your child. As parents, we tend to want to trust our children. Be aware, however, that parental trust can also be used by the enemy to access our children. We have to avoid the temptation of allowing trust to blind us to the possible negative consequences of undisciplined permissiveness. We should do everything we can to protect our children from dangers seen and unseen. Children are a blessing from God, and their personal welfare and spiritual development is our responsibility.

SPIRITUAL DEVELOPMENT FOR CHILDREN

Parents should be involved in their children's activities. However, recognizing that many parents leave the spiritual development of their children up to the church, it is vital that our church leaders understand the possible side effects of undisciplined permissiveness. Children should have safe, nurturing environments for learning. Youth ministers should develop curriculums and programs that are both fun and educational and that are designed to help children make godly choices.

It is important to teach children the truth about the consequences of ungodly choices. They should be taught discernment, because they may encounter ungodly people at school, at church, and possibly even at home. It is best to communicate openly with children, and especially with adolescents, about inappropriate sexual conduct.

If we are willing to share their struggles and create an environment at home and in church filled with encouragement, tenderness, patience, listening, affection, love, and faith in Christ Jesus, then we can teach children to place their trust in God and equip them with the power they need to withstand worldly pressures and ungodly manipulation.

However, if you respond to your children with sarcasm, destructive criticism, intimidation, fear, and unrealistic expectations, you may "provoke your children to wrath" rather than "bring[ing] them up in the training and admonition of the Lord" (Eph. 6:4, NKJV). Negative, harsh responses can incite children to become angry. Such behavior may cause them to seek love wherever they can find it. God wants us to nurture our children. They should be taught in an environment that is filled with love and the guidance of the Holy Spirit.

The Spirit of Truth Will Guide You

In her book *A Parents' Guide to Spiritual Warfare,* Leslie Montgomery provides insightful strategies to help parents combat spiritual attacks. She stresses the importance of teaching children to listen to the Holy Spirit for themselves so that they can respond to temptation in a godly way.[4] The Holy Spirit abides in all God's children and helps us to live godly lives. In John 16, Jesus tells us the Holy Spirit will guide believers "into all truth." The Holy Spirit empowers us to discern right and wrong. He wants to be involved in our lives. When we shut Him out, we leave ourselves open to listen to the deceiver.

If we teach our children about the Holy Spirit, then when they are confronted with sin they will know how to submit to

His warnings. They will make decisions based on biblical guidelines with a pure heart, a good conscience, and sincere faith. In *A Parents' Guide to Spiritual Warfare*, Leslie Montgomery writes, "When our children come face-to-face with sin, they have a choice: they can nurture it in order to fill a felt need, thereby eventually creating a stronghold for the enemy, or they can submit their felt needs to the Holy Spirit, who will fill that need with truth." She further explains, "When sin occurs—and it will—talk openly about what they are experiencing internally and how to correct the error. Our children must come to understand that to have the Holy Spirit with us and in us is a great privilege. It is also a great responsibility to listen to him and then respond in a godly way. When we ignore the Holy Spirit, we are ignoring God."[5]

The Holy Spirit is a precious gift. He will guide us into all truth and warn us against spiritual deception that can lead to apostasy. Grieving the Holy Spirit can give a foothold to the devil in our lives and cause us to forsake our faith. The apostle Paul understood the power and ability of the devil to tempt people, even believers, to turn away from God. In 1 Thessalonians 3:5, Paul writes about his concern for the Christians in the church at Thessalonica. Paul is anguished because Satan has prevented him from returning to Thessalonica (1 Thess. 2:18), and he is concerned for the faith of the people there. Paul understood the ungodly culture in which they lived. He did not want them to fall away due to the persecution they faced for going against tradition by accepting Christ.

We must teach our children about the Holy Spirit and welcome Him into our lives to guide us into all truth. As our children are led by the Holy Spirit, they will refrain from making decisions based on human judgment and instead learn to depend on His voice. In Zechariah 4:6, the Lord gives an instruction for human action that still applies today: "'Not by might nor by power, but by My Spirit,' Says the LORD of hosts" (NKJV). God's Holy Spirit sustains us with joy when we face spiritual opposition and gives us the power to stand in His might.

Live in Victory!

*J*ESUS DELEGATED HIS AUTHORITY TO us to retake the dominion that Adam and Eve had lost. He commanded us "to make disciples of all nations" (Matt. 28:18). Our mandate is no less than the social transformation of every community, neighborhood, county, city, region, and nation from the kingdom of darkness to the kingdom of God.

KINGDOM-MINDED

Our primary mission is to equip the saints to reclaim their lost inheritance. We must reclaim what is rightfully ours by taking dominion back from Satan. We are to be kingdom-minded, kingdom-focused, kingdom-motivated individuals whose primary goal in all that we do is advancing the kingdom of God.

Collectively, we have to broaden our focus from winning one soul at a time to converting entire nations. Every nation has areas that mold its culture. These areas—which have been referred to as the Seven Mountains because of their prominence in society—are religion, family, education, media, arts and entertainment, government, and business. Each of these mountains has someone at the top. To change the mountains, we need kingdom-minded, kingdom-motivated people at the top of them. According to Dr. C. Peter Wagner and Lance Wallnau, if Christians can gain influence over these Seven Mountains then entire nations can be changed.[1]

The Top of the Mountain

Transactions and negotiations are made at the top of each mountain that influence the entire mountain and, by extension, all of society. In order to transform our society and sustain the transformation permanently we must have a kingdom mentality ruling all the mountains. In America, Christians are primarily at the top of the mountain of religion. In the other mountains, however, Christians are generally at the bottom. How are we going to change this?

- Take the church to the workplace. (Many large companies have affinity groups where individuals bound by some common element can interact with one another—including a Christian group.)

- Intercede on behalf of mid-level Christian leaders so that they are included in corporate succession planning to be future leaders.

- Connect the Christian leaders of all seven mountains so that they are working in unison.

As a church, we collectively have to change from focusing only on the mountain of religion to focusing on transforming all seven mountains for the kingdom of God. It will not be easy, but through intercessory prayer and perseverance we can succeed. There is power in travailing prayer.

Travailing Prayer

The Lord spoke a word to me in a dream on February 8, 2008. He said, "Awakening baby first." I immediately awoke and wrote it down because in my spirit I knew it was very important. I thought about it throughout the day and prayed about it, asking the Lord to give me an understanding of what He meant. He gave me the answer the very next day. I had been studying about intercessory prayer, and one of the topics I came across was travailing prayer. Travailing prayer is earnest, heartfelt prayer. It is a deep, moaning-in-the-spirit, anguishing type of prayer. It happens when the person praying feels very deeply about something and is earnestly seeking God's help. It can be accompanied by fasting. Fasting and earnestly praying about something gets God's attention.

The Lord told me that "awakening baby first" meant, "Travailing prayer births the will of God on Earth. My purpose is to awaken the baby first. The spirit of slumber has a grip on the church (the baby) that has to be awakened (first) before the next move of God." This word from the Lord reveals how critical it is that Christians understand the impact prayer has on spiritual warfare. Prayer can change the spiritual atmosphere throughout the world and demolish the spiritual strongholds prevailing over the seven mountains.

Words of faith, love, and hope found in the Word of Truth can destroy every unrighteous stronghold and demonic structure. Strategic prayer is an essential antidote to the apathy that is subtly and slowly creeping across our nation. The church has the ability and spiritual power to fulfill Jesus' mandate to make disciples of all nations. It is time for the church to wake up and reclaim dominion!

THE ARMOR OF LIGHT

Christ will return to Earth for His church (Acts 1:9–11; Rev. 22). Until then, the church's role is to stand against evil, submit to God, and be a beacon for the world. Scripture tells us:

> And do this, understanding the present time. The hour has come for you to wake up from your slumber, because our salvation is nearer now than when we first believed. The night is nearly over; the day is almost here. So let us put aside the deeds of darkness and put on the armor of light. Let us behave decently, as in the daytime, not in orgies and drunkenness, not in sexual immorality and debauchery, not in dissension and jealousy. Rather, clothe yourselves with the Lord Jesus Christ, and do not think about how to gratify the desires of the sinful nature.
>
> —ROMANS 13:11–14

God wants the church to wake up spiritually and walk in the will, way, and works of the Lord. God tells us to put on the armor of light, meaning to be lampstands for the Lord, letting His light shine through our lifestyle so that others will see Christ in us and want to accept Jesus as their Lord. Jesus told Paul, "'I will rescue you from your own people and from the Gentiles. I am sending you to them to open their eyes and turn them from darkness to light, and from the power of Satan to God, so that they may receive forgiveness of sins and a place among those who are sanctified by faith in me'" (Acts 26:17–18). Jesus is the Light of the world (John 8:12; 9:5). He abides in all believers and wants us to let His light shine in order to draw others to Him.

When those we encounter are drawn to the Spirit of God in us, we will have an opportunity to talk about Jesus and minister to them by offering encouragement, strength, comfort, hope, and love. Jesus told us, "You are the light of the world....let your light shine before men, that they may see your good deeds and praise your Father in heaven" (Matt. 5:14, 16).

The church is responsible for preaching the full Word of

God—not a compromised version of the gospel—so that everyone will know why they need Jesus. Not only should the church preach God's promises, but it should also preach the consequences of sin. Yet, God's Word should be spoken in love. Rather than preaching "Turn (from sin) or Burn (in hell)" sermons, tell the world about the joy, peace, and happiness found in Jesus. Tell them about God's unconditional, endless love. God's grace is all-sufficient. He has "rescued us from the dominion of darkness and brought us into the kingdom of the Son he loves, in whom we have redemption, the forgiveness of sins" (Col. 1:13–14). Encourage one another and build each other up. Through Jesus we can become children of light (John 12:36). We can put aside our deeds of darkness, put on the armor of light, and be a symbol of hope to the world.

THE BATTLE IS NOW

The time to share the good news of the gospel is now. As a child, I sang a song in church called "I'm a Soldier in the Army of the Lord." I sang this song without truly understanding what it meant. And I certainly did not sing it with the idea of being a foot soldier in God's army who should be helping to develop strategies and plans to go into battle, much less to war. I suspect there are many Christians who sing battle songs each Sunday without understanding their significance. We tend to focus on the future battle that will take place when Jesus returns rather than on the present battle, the one that is taking place right here, right now.

A lack of spiritual wisdom and understanding has caused many of us to become blinded to the spiritual warfare that is taking place right now on Earth. We have become ineffective at recognizing the enemy and are not prepared to defend ourselves or our families. This shouldn't be the state in which we live. Scripture tells us:

> His divine power has given us *everything* we need for life and godliness through our knowledge of him who called us by his own glory and goodness. Through these he has given us his very great and precious promises, so that through them you may participate in the divine nature and escape the corruption in the world caused by evil desires.
> —2 Peter 1:3–4, emphasis added

We are told that God has given us everything we need to step into a life filled with His great and precious promises. We can escape the evil of this world if we have faith in God and His divine power. But faith must be more than belief in facts; it must result in action. God wants us to participate, not just sit on the sidelines. It's not too late to learn how to go to war with the enemy. Every Christian can become a soldier in the army of the Lord. Jesus promised that the gates of hell will not be able to prevail against His church (Matt. 16:18).

Fight in Unity with Authority

Christians have the power and authority in the name of Jesus to stand in the victory Jesus has already won (Matt. 28:18). Victory belongs to Christians because Christ abides in them as long as they keep His Word (John 14:20–21). Our victory begins with faith. We must first believe that God is God and that Jesus is His Son. Scripture tells us, "You believe that there is one God. You do well. Even the demons believe—and tremble!" (James 2:19, NKJV) The demons tremble because they know Jesus has triumphed over them. They know every Christian is able to stand in that victory and defeat them as well. However, we can only defeat them if we take action to do so. We must actively stand against the devil. The apostle James continues, "As the body without the spirit is dead, so faith without deeds is dead" (James 2:26). Faith produces action. We can act by putting on the full armor of God and by praying for all the saints (Eph. 6:1–18).

None of us can fight this war alone. We need to pray and get other people praying as well. We need to ask fellow Christians to help us with our battles by praying with us and for us. We must stand together in unity to keep the strong man out of our house. A unified church interceding through prayer, worship, praise, and love over a sustained period of time can effectively prevail against the enemy's attacks. We have power in the name of Jesus Christ, who is Lord over all (Eph. 1:21–23).

When we pray, our prayers should be based in God's Word, because God's Word reveals His will. Pray the answer, not the problem. For example, if you are feeling anxious or depressed about something, say, "Father, I thank you that I do not have a spirit of fear but of power and love and a sound mind" (based on 1 Tim. 1:7). When we pray according to His will, we know He hears us and we know we have what we ask of Him (1 John 5:14–15).

God is our heavenly Father. We can go to Him and talk to Him in the boldness that is our birthright as children of God. At times, boldness requires courage to press though our fears and do what we know is right. Faith's warfare sometimes requires prayer that, because we don't know what to pray for, is beyond our ability. It is in these times that we should "pray in the Spirit" as the apostle Paul instructs us (Eph. 6:18). Likewise, the Holy Spirit helps us in our weaknesses and intercedes for us according to the will of God (Rom. 8:26–28). The Holy Spirit will help us to pray over every situation that arises in our life. Serious prayer requires concentration. It puts us in focus with God's will, which is revealed in God's Word. It can change us, and it can change our situations.

Intercessory prayer is a mighty weapon to use against the enemy. It can be used both before and during an attack. Parents frequently pray a hedge of protection around their children to protect them from dangers seen and unseen. Intercessors frequently pray the prayer of faith with the sick, healing them in the process (James 5:14–15). Prayer provides comfort and support. Prayer can be used to fortify and strengthen each other. Our prayers build our faith, because when they are answered we can see tangible evidence that God hears us.

STRATEGIC CORPORATE SPIRITUAL WARFARE

The National Day of Prayer in America is set aside to combat the sociocultural aspect of spiritual warfare (the supernatural forces of evil that manipulate institutions, governments, and social structures to advance ungodly principles). This annual day of intercession has been established because Scripture tells us that "the effective, fervent prayer of the righteous avails much" (James 5:16, NKJV). Prayer warriors nationwide pray for a spiritual atmosphere that will influence our leaders and communities to support godly practices and beliefs. And when necessary, they pray for God to intervene to overthrow ungodly laws.

Travailing prayer and supplication in the Holy Spirit is a powerful method of activating the divine power needed to demolish the demonic strongholds found in the sociocultural realm of spiritual warfare. For example, some people want to remove the phrase "In God We Trust" from U.S. currency. In the natural realm, this may not seem like a big deal. However, in the spirit realm, this would be a major victory for Satan and could signal to God that we as a nation no longer place our trust in Him. Prayer warriors understand the significance of trusting in God and keeping His hand of protection on us as a nation. The National Day of Prayer is used to amass an army of prayer warriors to stand together against ungodly tenets that can affect our nation.

Cindy Jacobs, author of *Possessing the Gates of the Enemy,* has mobilized intercessors worldwide to pray strategically to overthrow Satan's thrones of iniquity. Her book is a training manual for militant intercession. In it, she teaches us that we are called to intercede in order to "wage war in the heavenlies."[2] God responds to prayer. Prayer in the authority we have in the name of Jesus can alter the spiritual atmosphere of our nation and of the world and can penetrate and destroy the enemy's demonic strongholds.

Effective strategic spiritual warfare requires a coordinated, united front designed to attack the enemy from every angle to overthrow his strongholds. At the individual church level, it can begin with identifying a problem or a concern and then asking God for strategic spiritual revelation and guidance on how to overthrow the enemy in this matter. It is important to get the entire church involved because, as with any battle, there is strength in numbers.

Sometimes it can be difficult to know how to get started, so I offer the following twelve-day prayer for guidance. Twelve is a number that signifies union, oneness. By joining together and praying in unison and agreement, we can all do our part to actively bring down the demonic forces that are attempting to stop the advancement of the kingdom of God.

TWELVE-DAY PRAYER TO BRING DOWN DEMONIC FORCES

Day 1

Begin by praying for your home and family. Pray a hedge of protection around them. Pray that no weapon formed against you will prosper (Isa. 54:17). Declare, "As for me and my household, we will serve the LORD" (Josh. 24:15). Read Psalm 91.

Day 2

Pray for the area in which you live. God placed you in your city or area of the country for a purpose, as we are told in the Book of Acts: "And He has made from one blood every nation of men to dwell on all the face of the earth, and has determined their preappointed times and the boundaries of their dwellings" (Acts 17:26, NKJV). Pray for the breaking of demonic strongholds in your area and in the whole nation. Read John 17.

Day 3

Pray for spiritual discernment. Pray "that the God of our Lord Jesus Christ, the Father of glory, may give to you the spirit of wisdom and revelation in the knowledge of Him, the eyes of your understanding being enlightened; that you may know what is the hope of His calling, what are the riches of the glory of His inheritance in the saints, and what is the exceeding greatness of His power toward us who believe, according to the working of His mighty power" (Eph. 1:17–19, NKJV). Read Ephesians 1 and 3. Memorize Proverbs 3:5–6.

Day 4

Pray for your church and all Christian churches; pray for religious freedom and the destruction of antichrist systems. Pray for the removal of the spiritual blinders that the enemy has wrapped around the minds of unbelievers everywhere—those "whose minds the god of this age has blinded, who do not believe" (2 Cor. 4:4, NKJV). Read 2 Corinthians 4.

Day 5

Pray to thwart the plans of the enemy. Pray to bring down witchcraft and all forms of the occult that God hates. Satan and his spirit of deception are using entertainment such as *Sabrina the Teenage Witch* to lure our world and especially our youth into thinking that witchcraft is fun and acceptable. The Pentagon allows Wiccans to worship openly on military bases. Deuteronomy 18:9–12 warns: "Thou shalt not learn to do after the abominations of those nations. There shall not be found among you any one...that useth divination, or an observer of times, or an enchanter, or a witch. Or a charmer, or a consulter with familiar spirits, or a wizard, or a necromancer. For all that do these things are an abomination unto the LORD" (KJV). Read Jeremiah 29 and 1 John 4.

Day 6

Pray for the breaking and binding of all evil spirits, and especially the spirit of slumber in our churches and the spirits of deception and of pride. Read Psalm 37 and Ezekiel 34.

Day 7

Pray that God's "will be done on earth as it is in heaven" (Matt. 6:10). Pray, "And this is my prayer: that [my] love may abound more and more in knowledge and depth of insight, so that [I] may be able to discern what is best and may be pure and blameless until the day of Christ, filled with the fruit of righteousness that comes through Jesus Christ—to the glory and praise of God" (Phil. 1:9–11). Read Philippians 1 and 2.

Day 8

Pray for your church leaders specifically and all church leaders in general, that they may know that their labor is worthwhile. "Therefore, my dear brothers [and sisters], stand firm. Let nothing move you. Always give yourselves fully to the work of the Lord, because you know that your labor in the Lord is not in vain" (1 Cor. 15:58). Read 2 Corinthians 1 and 2.

Day 9

Pray for apostles, prophets, pastors, and teachers. Pray that they are not misled or deceived by the spirit of deception. Pray that they "preach the Word; [are] prepared in season and out of season; [and] correct, rebuke and encourage—with great patience and careful instruction" (2 Tim. 4:2). Read 2 Timothy 3 and 4.

Day 10

Pray for evangelists and missionaries, those who are living out the commandment to "'go into all the world and preach the good news to all creation'" (Mark 16:15). Read Acts 2 and 7 and Romans 12.

Day 11

Pray for intercessors, watchmen, God's army, and warriors. Read Ezekiel 33. Also read 2 Corinthians 1:11, 2 Corinthians 9:14, and Philippians 1:4 for examples of how Christians should pray for each other.

Day 12

Pray for the baptism of the Holy Spirit and for spiritual gifts. Read Acts 1 and 1 Corinthians 12.

Plan to have a powerfully joyful praise and worship service at the conclusion of the twelve-day prayer cycle. Come before the Lord with thanksgiving. Thank the Lord for hearing and answering your prayers! Recite Psalm 100 out loud: "Make a joyful noise unto the LORD, all ye lands. Serve the LORD with gladness: come before his presence with singing. Know ye that the LORD he is God: it is he that hath made us, and not we ourselves; we are his people, and the sheep of his pasture. Enter into his gates with thanksgiving, and into his courts with praise: be thankful unto him, and bless his name. For the LORD is good; his mercy is everlasting; and his truth endureth to all generations" (KJV). Give a shout to the Lord!

MORE THAN CONQUERORS!

In Hosea 4:6, the Lord tells us, "My people are destroyed for lack of knowledge" (KJV). One of the purposes of this book is to offer spiritual knowledge to open your eyes to the truth so that with your eyes wide open, staring down the enemy, you can defeat him when he sends an attack against you or someone you love. You can join God's army to overthrow the enemy by learning the principles of effective strategic spiritual warfare. Only then can you truly sing, "I am a soldier in the army of the Lord."

I began this book by asking if you are living your life in the Matrix, blinded to the spiritual battle that is taking place every day and that is influencing your day-to-day decisions. Some of you may still not believe in the biblical principle of spiritual warfare or that the manifestation of supernatural forces in the earthly realm is possible. However, if you can bring yourself to ask God for spiritual discernment, then you won't be one of the ones who perishes for lack of knowledge.

Throughout this book, I have continued to ask two questions: Who is in control of your life? and, Is it possible that you are not in control? These questions are asked with the intent of opening your eyes to the possibility of the manifestation of spiritual warfare in the earthly realm so that you can see how it can impact your day-to-day decisions. Once you accept the possibility, you can learn how to align your decisions with godly wisdom and can successfully battle these spiritual forces of evil and live your life in victory through Christ Jesus.

As believers, we have victory over the spirit world. We have the following assurance:

> Who shall separate us from the love of Christ? shall tribulation, or distress, or persecution, or famine, or nakedness, or peril, or sword?...Nay, in all these things we are more than conquerors through him that loved us. For I am persuaded, that neither death, nor life, nor angels, nor principalities, nor powers, nor things present, nor things to come, Nor height, nor depth, nor any other creature, shall be able to separate us from the love of God, which is in Christ Jesus our Lord.
>
> —ROMANS 8:35, 37–39, KJV

Through Jesus and the power of the Holy Spirit, we can take our stand against the enemy, live victorious lives, and possess our rightful inheritance from God!

Salvation Prayer

Heavenly Father, it is written in Your Holy Word that if I confess with my mouth that Jesus is Lord and I believe in my heart that You raised Jesus from the dead, then I shall be saved. Father, I confess that Jesus is my Lord. I make Him Lord of my life right now. I believe in my heart that You raised Your Son, Jesus, from the dead. I renounce my past life with Satan and close the door to all his devices. I thank You for forgiving me of all my sins and for saving me. Jesus is my Lord! In the name of Jesus I pray. Amen.

Notes

INTRODUCTION

1. Francis Bacon, "The Advancement of Learning," *Works of Lord Bacon, Part 1* (Whitefish, MT: Kessinger, 2003), 75, GoogleBooks, http://books.google.com/books?id=31tPGUbSFdIC&pg=PA75&lpg=PA75&dq=#v=onepage&q=&f=false, accessed March 16, 2010.

2. Blaise Pascal, *Pensées* (Charleston, SC: BiblioBazaar, 2008), 14, GoogleBooks, http://books.google.com/books?id=HXX64CpdaicC&pg=PA14&lpg=PA14#v=onepage&q=&f=false, accessed March 16, 2010.

CHAPTER 1

1. Aristotle, *Posterior Analytics* (Whitefish, MT: Kessinger, 2004), Book 2, Part 2, GoogleBooks, http://books.google.com/books?id=sSpixzDAkF8C&printsec=frontcover&dq=aristotle+posterior+analytics&source=#v=onepage&q=&f=false, accessed March 19, 2010.

2. Thomas Aquinas, *Summa Theologiae* (London: Blackfriars, 1963), Preface, vol. 1, xi.

3. Ibid., Ia, Qu. 2, art. 3, vol. 2.

4. Ibid.

5. Anthony Thiselton, *A Concise Encyclopedia of the Philosophy of Religion* (Oxford: OneWorld Publications, 2002), 45, 103.

6. Ibid., 45.

7. Fritz Heider, *The Psychology of Interpersonal Relations* (Hillsdale, NJ: Lawrence Erlbaum Associates, 1958), 1.

8. J. A. Bargh and E. Morsella, "The Unconscious Mind," *Perspectives on Psychological Science: A Journal of the Association for Psychological Science* 3, no. 1 (2008): 3, 73–79, http://www.yale.edu/acmelab/articles/Bargh_Morsella_Unconscious_Mind.pdf.

9. J. A. Bargh, ACME Lab Web site, Yale University, http://www.yale.edu/acmelab/, accessed March 29, 2010.

10. Benedict Carey, "Who's Minding the Mind," *New York Times*, July 31, 2007, Ibid.

11. Ibid.

12. Ibid.

13. D. Gandy and M. Clark, *Choose! The Role That Choice Plays In Shaping Women's Lives* (Dallas, TX: Brown Book Publishing Group, 2004).

14. Bernard Madoff, "Plea Allocution of Bernard Madoff," *Wall Street Journal*, March 12, 2009, http://online.wsj.com/public/resources/documents/20090315madoffall.pdf, accessed March 12, 2009.

15. *The American Heritage College Dictionary, Fourth Edition* (Boston-New York: Houghton Mifflin Company, 2007), s.v. "free will."

CHAPTER 2

1. *The American Heritage College Dictionary* (Boston-New York: Houghton Mifflin Company, 1981), s.v. "emotion."

2. Ibid., s.v. "phobia."

3. Catholic Pro-Life Committee, www.prolifedallas.org, accessed March 10, 2009.

4. *Roe v. Wade*, 410 U.S. 113, 117.

5. Ibid., 148.

6. Ibid.

7. Ibid., 149.

8. Ibid., 151.

9. Ibid., 160.

10. "*Roe v. Wade*," *Wikipedia*, http://en.wikipedia.org/wiki/Roe_v._Wade, accessed March 29, 2010.

11. Ibid.

12. Ibid.

13. Ibid.

14. *McCorvey v. Hill, 385 F.3d 846,* Fifth Circuit Court of Appeals No. 03-10711, September 17, 2004, http://www.ca5.uscourts.gov/opinions%5Cpub%5C03/03-10711-CV0.wpd.pdf, accessed March 21, 2010.

15. "Mother Confesses to Severing Baby's Arms," Associated Press, MSNBC.com, November 23, 2004, http://www.msnbc.msn.com/id/6561617/, accessed March 21, 2010.

16. "Plano Mom Who Cut Off Baby's Arms to Be Released," CBS 11 Dallas, November 7, 2008, www.cbs11tv.com, accessed March 5, 2009.

17. Lisa Sweetingham, "Andrea Yates found not guilty by reason of insanity in children's death," CourtTV, July 26, 2006, CourtTVnews.com, accessed March 5, 2009.

18. "University shooter interested in 'peace and social justice,'" CNN. com, http://www.cnn.com/2008/US/02/15/university.shooting.suspect/index.html?eref=yahoo, accessed March 5, 2009.

19. *Microsoft Encarta Dictionary*, Windows Vista Home 2007, accessed via Microsoft Word Research Tools, s.v., "evil."

CHAPTER 3

1. *The Usual Suspects*, dir. Brian Singer, writer Christopher McQuarrie, Grammercy Pictures, Hollywood, 2005.

2. *Microsoft Encarta Dictionary*, s.v., "naturalism."

3. *Strong's Concordance* (Nashville, TN: Thomas Nelson, 1995), s.v. "Maveth: Hebrew 4194."

4. "The Founders of Wicca in the United States," *Church and School of Wicca*, www.wicca.org, accessed April 9, 2009.

5. "New Age Spirituality," *Religious Tolerance,* http://www.religioustolerance.org/newage.htm, accessed April 13, 2009.

6. *The American Heritage College Dictionary,* s.v. "pantheism."

7. "New Age Spirituality," *Religious Tolerance.*

8. "Yoga," *Wikipedia*, http://en.wikipedia.org/wiki/Yoga, accessed June 16, 2009.

9. Ed Murphy, *Handbook for Spiritual Warfare* (Nashville, TN: Thomas Nelson, 2003).

10. Ibid.

11. C.H. Kraft, *Defeating Dark Angels: Breaking Demonic Oppression in the Believer's Life* (Ventura, CA: Regal Books, 1992), 44.

12. Ibid., 102–111.

CHAPTER 4

1. *The American Heritage College Dictionary*, s.v. "spirit" and "soul."

2. C. Peter Wagner and Robert Henderson, "PW822 Divine Healing," April 2008, *Healing in the Perspective of the Kingdom of God,* Online Wagner Leadership Institute class.

3. Chuck D. Pierce and Rebecca Wagner Systema, *The Future War of the Church* (Ventura, CA: Regal Books, 2007).

4. *The American Heritage College Dictionary*, s.v. "anti."

5. Ibid., s.v. "Antichrist."

6. Ibid., s.v. "system."

7. "Christian Persecution in India Continues," *Christianity Today* online, March 6, 2005, http://www.christiantoday.com/article/christian.persecution.in.india.continues./2273.htm, accessed May 26, 2009.

8. "Globally Persecution Has Increased," *Christian Persecution Info*, www.christianpersecution.info, accessed March 29, 2010.

9. "India: Christians attacked in Karanataka, India," Compass Direct News, September 10, 2008, *Christian Persecution*, http://www.christianpersecution.info/news/india-christians-attacked-in-karanataka-india-16206/, accessed May 26, 2009

10. *American Heritage College Dictionary*, s.v. "enmity."

11. *Strong's Concordance*, s.v., "Apeithes: Greek 545."

12. *Life Application Study Bible, New International Version edition* (Wheaton, IL: Tyndale House and Zondervan, 1997), s.v., "Matt. 15:22–23."

Chapter 5

1. Tim Rowe, *The Magnificent Goodness of God* (Xulon, 2009).

2. *300*, dir. Zack Snyder, Warner Brothers Pictures, Hollywood, 2007.

3. *Strong's Concordance*, s.v., "perissos."

4. John Keller with Margie Knight, *A Miracle on the Road to Recovery* (Tulsa, OK: Word and Spirit Resources, 2010), back cover.

5. Ronnie Moore, *Ministry of the Holy Spirit in the Last Days* (Hurst, TX: Ronnie Moore Ministries, 2006), 35.

6. "Purgatory," *Wikipedia*, http://en.wikipedia.org/wiki/Purgatory, accessed May 30, 2009.

7. Ibid.

8. Moore, *Ministry of the Holy Spirit in the Last Days*, 35.

9. Kenneth E. Hagin, *The Believer's Authority* (Tulsa, OK: Kenneth Hagin Ministries, 2005).

10. Ibid.

Chapter 6

1. Margaret Thatcher, quoted at ThinkExist.com, http://thinkexist.com/quotation/you_may_have_to_fight_a_battle_more_than_once_to/11470.html, accessed March 18, 2010.

2. "President Clinton's Letter to Congress: Cloning Prohibiton Act," June 9, 1997, The White House Office of the Press Secretary, http://clinton3.nara.gov/New/Remarks/Mon/19970609-15987.html, accessed May 30, 2009.

3. "President Bush on Cloning," *Newshour with Jim Lehrer—OnLine Newshour,* April 10, 2002, http://www.pbs.org/newshour/updates/april02/bush-cloning_4-10.html, accessed May 30, 2009.

4. "President Clinton's Letter to Congress: Cloning Prohibiton Act."

5. "Obama Reverses Bush-era Stem-Cell Policy," Associated Press, March 9, 2009, MSNBC.com, http://www.msnbc.msn.com/id/29586269/, accessed May 29, 2009.

6. "Full Text: President Obama Speech on Stem Cell Policy Change," White House Press Office, March 9, 2009, *Clips and Comment,* http://www.clipsandcomment.com/2009/03/09/full-text-president-obama-speech-on-stem-cell-policy-change/, accessed May 29, 2009.

7. "Obama Reverses Bush-era Stem-Cell Policy."

8. "Full Text: President Obama Speech on Stem Cell Policy Change."

9. Ed Silvoso, *That None Should Perish* (Ventura, CA: Regal Books, 1994).

10. Germaine Copeland, *Prayers That Avail Much* (Tulsa, OK: Harrison House, 2000).

Chapter 7

1. *Strong's Concordance,* s.v., *"esomai:* Greek 2071."

2. Louis J. Freeh, "A Parent's Guide to Internet Safety," U.S. Dept of Justice—Federal Bureau of Investigation (FBI), http://www.fbi.gov/publications/pguide/pguidee.htm, accessed June 1, 2009.

3. Ibid.

4. Leslie Montgomery, *A Parents' Guide to Spiritual Warfare* (Wheaton, IL: Crossway Books, 2006).

5. Ibid.

Chapter 8

1. Dr. C. Peter Wagner, "The 7-M Mandate," Global Harvest's Global Congress *From Intercession to Declaration: Warring with the Word of God,* Denton, Texas, September 14, 2007.

2. Cindy Jacobs, *Possessing the Gates of the Enemy* (Grand Rapids, MI: Chosen Books, 2006).

Additional Resources

1. Charles Stanley, *Protecting Your Family* (Nashville, TN: Thomas Nelson, Inc., 1998).

2. Chip Ingram, *The Invisible War* (Grand Rapids, MI: Baker Books, 2006).

To Contact the Author

LIFENMATRX@YAHOO.COM